19

Community Planning in the 1920's

Community Plannin

the 1920's:

*The Contribution of the
Regional Planning
Association of America*

BY ROY LUBOVE

Library of Congress Catalog Number 64–12492
© 1963 University of Pittsburgh Press

TO MY FATHER AND THE
MEMORY OF MY MOTHER

Preface

To stress the significance of housing and community planning to the field of social welfare would seem unnecessary. Yet neither has received sufficient research or policy attention within the ranks of the social professions. Certainly, few issues today are of more moment than the nature of our conditioning environment. What kinds of communities best serve our needs? Should they be planned, and if so, who shall plan them? Who shall live in them? Where should communities be located? What resources should they contain? These are but a few of the questions of social policy relating to community organization and affecting a breadth of contemporary problems from civil rights to mental health and family life. The contemporary emphasis on the phenomenon of anomie symbolizes the social impact of the community.

Despite the relatively lengthy history of planning, our society is hardly at the threshold of a rational approach to community development. A glance backwards may help us to recognize some of the obstacles over which we have stumbled and which continue to block our path. For example, to what extent have community goals been determined by romantic visions of the past rather than projections of the future? How often has reform been inspired by a negative attitude toward the city as a way of life? Thoreau would find more followers in the twentieth-century city than he had in his rustic New England. Looking backward has been a perennial failing of the community reformer.

At other times the means of achievement have been anachronistic. As Dr. Lubove's study documents, reliance on the speculative housing industry has been less than successful in meeting the housing needs of our citizenry. The private market has rarely provided adequately for a considerable portion of our population. Differing from other mass products, housing has not become more available to lower income customers through lower prices resulting from increased rationalization of production. Yet housing policy continues to favor private housing over a variety of alternatives which have been successful in other countries. Under these circumstances can we expect to be a well-housed nation?

Particularly noteworthy in the past was the effort of the Regional Planning Association of America to make community planning an integrated discipline, one combining the physical and the social. This effort seems not to have laid the seeds for later growth. The physical planners, on the whole, took the initiative but the social planners hardly entered the field. While it might be said that social policy in housing and community development has not been encouraged by those in control, it might equally be contended that social scientists and the social professions have offered all too little to be given serious consideration. Most frequently their major efforts, rather than constructive and progressive, have been concentrated on condemning the more obvious inequities of the past. For clues to action we might well turn to Clarence Stein, one of the most influential figures cited by Dr. Lubove. Trained in architecture, Stein cooperated with settlement workers and in the 1920's combined the promotion of good housing and good communities with a concern for the needs of low-income groups.

Physical planners have differed in the degree to which they have accepted responsibility for determining the direction of community development, but some, like those of the Regional Planning Association of America, have faced their tasks with a greater sense of freedom and frankness than their social counterparts. The members of the RPAA envisioned a variety of life styles corresponding to a variety of community types; and they harnessed imagination to science in determining the conditions for urban progress. A similar approach on the part of the social policy specialists might contribute significantly to the development of community planning.

From the point of view of the strategist of action as well as of the planner, the opportunity to examine an important phase of the history of community planning is of great value. Hopefully, it will point toward more rational policy-making in this vitally important field.

SAMUEL MENCHER
University of Pittsburgh

Contents

Introduction

THE FORMATION of the Regional Planning Association of America (RPAA) in 1923 signified a sharp break with traditional housing and
planning objectives in the United States. Composed
of a small number of architects, planners, and social
critics in full rebellion against metropolitan centralization and suburban diffusion alike, the RPAA proposed an alternative best described as community
planning. Frequent identification of the RPAA with
the Garden City and urban decentralization has
obscured its community planning synthesis—its
search for the basic principles underlying good urban
residential environment and, more generally, the
urban structure best suited to the satisfaction of
human biological and social needs.

The RPAA viewed residential environment as a
function of creative site-planning and economical
subdivision involving large-scale units like the superblock, the neighborhood, and even whole communities; cost analysis with special reference to the supply
of low-interest capital; and regional planning directed toward the nurture of multiple community-

types. The community planning efforts of the RPAA represented a memorable experiment in coordinated physical and social planning and a significant attempt to discover and integrate into a single program the variables affecting urban residential environment.

In working out its community planning program, the RPAA did not seek to impose any special urban form or container such as the Garden City. It viewed Ebenezer Howard's classic formulation not as a plan to be applied literally and mechanically like the rectangular subdivision but as a clue to a new urban orientation and structure: quantum or unit development incorporating most necessary attributes of urban life in contrast to fragmented metropolitan accretion or suburban diffusion, and optimum urban size expressed as a function of desired social or community relationships and goals. The regional city idea involved far more than the creation of Garden Cities or New Towns. It implied the preservation of the integrity of small towns and villages as well as the reconstruction and renewal of metropolitan centers. Thus the regional city as understood by the RPAA should not suggest a single, arbitrary form, nor a low-density dispersion, nor the break-up of metropolitan agglomerations, but rather a flexible, experimental effort to achieve a satisfactory regional balance of population, resources, and institutions.

In reviewing the American past, the RPAA uncovered few precedents for its community planning synthesis. A number of partial expressions had appeared—the New England colonial farm village, the romantic pedestrian-scale suburbs of Frederick Law

Olmsted at Riverside, Illinois, and Roland Park near Baltimore, the superior examples of industrial town planning like Pullman, Illinois, and Kingsport, Tennessee, and the federal housing program of World War I. Members of the RPAA found nothing at all to commend in the dominant nineteenth- and early twentieth-century tradition of housing betterment through minimum standards legislation. However, a small community planning experiment, all but forgotten by the 1920's, had occurred in Lowell, Massachusetts, linking the pre-World War I Progressive reform movement with the efforts of the RPAA in the 1920's to improve residential environment through innovations in design, finance, and planning.

The city on the Merrimack—whose cotton mills, boardinghouses, and genteel female operatives had attracted international renown in the mid-nineteenth century by demonstrating, ostensibly, that industrialization did not necessarily result in social degradation—was selected by the Massachusetts Homestead Commission (MHC) in 1917 as the site for America's first "public housing" development. The Commission erected only a few homes, but these represented the culmination of almost a decade's effort by reformers dissatisfied with the results of restrictive housing legislation and critical of city planning schemes which ignored fundamental questions of low-cost housing supply and social environment. The Lowell experiment did not consciously influence the members of the RPAA, but it is worth examining, nonetheless, as an episode which foreshadowed the new perspective on housing and planning which emerged in the 1920's. Even before World War I a nucleus of reformers felt that restrictive legislation represented an inadequate response to the problems of housing supply and residential environment in the urban setting.

Chapter 1

THE MASSACHUSETTS LEGISLATURE had originally authorized the appointment of a tempo-
rary Homestead Commission in 1909 to consider
"whether it would be expedient for the Commonwealth to acquire or open for settlement lands in
country districts with the view of aiding honest,
industrious and ambitious families of wage-earners
to remove thereto from congested tenement districts
of the various large cities and towns. . . ." [1] Although urged to recommend such a program by
Massachusetts labor leaders and by Representative
James H. Mellen of Worcester, who had been responsible for its appointment, the Commission majority delivered a negative report. A minority report,
however, was prepared by Freeman M. Saltus of
Worcester, who proposed state acquisition of large
tracts of land, their subdivision into smaller tracts
of one and one-half to two acres, and state erection
of cottages for wage earners. The House Committee
on Public Health prepared a bill based upon Saltus'
recommendations, but it was tabled by the Committee on Ways and Means. [2]

Despite the initial defeat in 1910, Mellen continued to press for homestead legislation, and in 1911 the legislature authorized the appointment of another commission to prepare a plan enabling workers to acquire small houses and garden plots with Commonwealth assistance. The governor appointed three members of this Commission: Eva W. White, a Boston social worker; Warren D. Foster, a lawyer; and Henry Sterling, a Medford labor leader. Its ex officio members included Charles F. Gettemy, director of the Bureau of Statistics of Labor; Arthur B. Chapin, Bank Commissioner; Keynon L. Butterfield, president of the Massachusetts Agricultural College; and Clement F. Coogan, of the State Board of Health. Sterling was elected secretary of the Commission and assumed the lead in shaping its program.[3]

Between 1911 and its demise in 1919, the MHC labored to redirect the flow of population from the cities of the state to the suburbs and country. In pursuing this goal, it devoted considerable attention to the kind of housing most suitable for those workers who wished to escape the congested urban centers, to the problem of financing this reverse migration, and to city planning procedures which promised to improve the general character of residential environments throughout the state. The Commission's long-range, comprehensive housing program, concerned with matters of design and site-planning, state financing, city planning, and a kind of regional planning aimed at rejuvenating country life, distinguished its work from that of contemporary housing reformers who limited themselves to restrictive legislation and ineffectual proposals for garden cities and villages. The superiority ascribed by the Commission to the single-family detached house, as opposed to the multi-family tenement, greatly influenced its thinking, as did the assumption that contact with nature was indispensable to a humane existence. In the eyes of the Commission, the private home and exposure to nature were sources of physical and moral well-being, and the state's surest guarantee of good citizenship. These normative judgments underlay the Commission's program and shaped its fundamental conclusion that neither commercial builders nor limited-dividend model tenement companies had thus far satisfied the housing needs of lower-income groups. Objecting that a "large portion of the money invested in improved housing conditions has been used in erecting tenements," the Commission argued that these were hardly superior to the commercial tenement and, more important, that widespread tenement development of any type simply demonstrated the failure of private enterprise to meet its responsibilities to the worker and the state.[4]

In a report to the legislature in January 1912, the MHC requested authority to purchase one or more tracts of land on which to erect wage-earners' homes. It suggested that the project be financed by loans from unclaimed funds of savings banks deposited with the treasurer of the Commonwealth. The scheme failed when the Massachusetts Supreme Court, in a preliminary opinion, ruled the bill unconstitutional. The legislature thereupon directed the Commission to continue its investigations into the housing problem, which resulted in a report in January 1913 evaluating the relationship between city planning and housing. Always alert to developments abroad, the Commission explained that planning had been accepted as a necessity in all those foreign communities which had become "more healthful and more desirable places to live." The Commission deplored the fact that American cities grew haphazardly when even a fence or ditch required some measure of planning and forethought. Attributing "disease, poverty, ignorance, vice, and crime" to the "haphazard, unsystematic development of our cities, and the selfish utilization of their natural resources, and the resultant conditions of lack of room, air and sunlight in congested tenement districts," the Commission recommended the mandatory establishment of planning boards in all communities containing 10,000 or more inhabitants.[5] The subsequent Massachusetts planning act of 1913 was almost entirely attributable to the initiative of the MHC, which espoused a lofty ideal of the planning function:

The specific aim of city planning is to promote health, convenience and beauty in the city, thereby conserving human life and energy. Such planning concerns itself with all the physical aspects of the city or town,—its streets, railroads and waterways, its public services, its administrative, educational and recreative property,—treating them as component parts of an organic whole, so that each may dovetail into the next.[6]

The fact that twenty-four cities had established planning boards by the end of 1913 no doubt gratified the Commission, but it still lacked authority for dealing directly with the housing problem. The only recourse was a constitutional amendment permitting the state to engage in housing activities. Prepared by the Commission, an enabling amendment was approved by the legislature in 1914 and 1915, and ratified by the voters in the state elections of 1915. It gave the General Court power to purchase and improve land in order to relieve congestion and provide homes for citizens, provided, however, that neither land nor buildings were sold below cost.[7] Although denied an appropriation in 1916, the MHC received $50,000 the following year for a projected fifty-home development in Lowell.

The historic Lowell experiment, which ultimately produced only twelve homes, represented the contribution of reformers who utilized progressive means to accomplish conservative, traditional ends. Beneath the Commission's protests against congested urban slums and their physical and social ills ran an undercurrent of rebellion against the entire urbanization process of the previous half-century. It was a source of deep regret to the Commission that the portion of the state's population residing in towns of less than 5,000 population decreased from one-half in 1850 to one-eighth in 1910. In the larger cities into which immigrants and country population streamed, builders erected "cheap tenements and workingmen's barracks with their accompanying evils, squalor and vitiating influences." This floating tenement population possessed only an "ephemeral" interest in the welfare of the community. It consisted of nomads whose mode of existence acted to the "detriment of public health, standards of life, ideals and morals."[8] The congested tenement slums of the large cities represented a serious "social disease," according to one member of the Commission, and the cure lay in state action designed to "take families from the congested districts, plant them in small houses, detached or otherwise, but with a garden plot, and give them a real chance in the fresh air and sunshine, with dirt to dig in and to grow things in, and with outdoors for the children to play in, and with a stake in the world." [9]

Far from being an appendage, the garden plot attached to the home was central to the Commission's entire program and social philosophy. "It would be impossible to imagine a strong and energetic race," the Commission insisted, "coming from generations habituated only to contact with stone pavements, wooden floors and brick walls." Tenement restrictions upon light, fresh air, privacy, and play space for children sapped the "vitality of the race" and precluded the "upbuilding of a virile people." [10] The Commission maintained, however, that farming and gardening required training and experience; it did not intend simply to supply urban workers with land or equipment which would prove useless. A "back-to-the-soil" movement depended upon opportunities for agricultural education, and in 1916 the MHC induced the legislature to enact a measure authorizing cities to establish schools of agriculture and horticulture. The Commission was convinced that with proper instruction, supervision, and "if need be, some compulsion," families residing in state-financed homes could appreciably increase their incomes through intensive garden cultivation. [11]

The resettlement visions of the MHC were in-

spired, in part, by the liberal federal land policies of
the nineteenth century which culminated in the original Homestead Act of 1862. Important also was
the "country life" movement of the early twentieth
century, in which Kenyon L. Butterfield, a member
of the Commission, played a leading role. Active as
a teacher and editor in Michigan agricultural affairs
in the 1890's and a member of Theodore Roosevelt's
Country Life Commission, Butterfield was regarded
as a leading authority on rural sociology and community organization. But, in developing a concrete
resettlement program using state capital, the Commission relied more upon foreign than American experience. It compiled extensive data on foreign land
and housing legislation in an effort to determine the
proper function and responsibility of the state.

The Commission contended, in light of its preference for the private house, countryside, and soil,
that commercial enterprise had failed to meet the
housing needs of low-income groups in Europe as
well as America. It criticized the United States, however, as one of the few "civilized nations" whose
government refrained from actively aiding and en-
couraging the "creation of a larger supply of good
homes." Central, state, and local authorities in
Europe, the Commission pointed out, had adopted
various expedients—tax exemption, government
housing, low-interest loans to consumers—in an effort to increase the quantity of good, low-cost housing. The same was true of New Zealand and Australia, whose government land and housing policies
exerted the greatest single influence upon the MHC.
In these outposts of Western civilization, according

to Henry Sterling who compiled the Commission's data, "the more popular idea seems to be to promote and encourage a 'back-to-the-land' movement." [12]

American proponents of country life and a resettlement program intended to restrain the tide of urbanization had good reason to look enviously at the land and housing policies of New Zealand and Australia. Beginning in the early 1890's, New Zealand had enacted legislation designed to break up large estates and transfer the land to small settlers on liberal credit terms. Thus the Land for Settlements Acts authorized an expenditure of $2,500,000 yearly (increased to $5,000,000 in 1900) towards the purchase of estates by mutual agreement or compulsory sale. An Advances to Settlers Act of 1894 provided for loans to settlers ranging from $125 to $15,000, repayable at 3 per cent over a thirty-six-and-one-half-year period. A Land Settlement Finance Act of 1909 enabled groups of settlers to purchase private tracts of land, raising the capital through government-insured loans. A Workers' Dwellings Act of 1906 provided for the erection of cottages on crown or private lands, and an Advances to Workers Act of 1906 authorized loans to workers for the building or purchase of homes. Between 1893 and 1912 New Zealand spent more than $32,000,000 to acquire more than 1,350,000 acres of land, and it authorized more than $10,000,000 worth of loans in connection with the Advances to Workers Act.

The Australian states aided settlers and workers through similar legislation. Queensland's Closer Settlement Act of 1906 provided for crown purchase of land, the laying out roads and townships, and distribution of the remaining land to settlers. A Workers' Dwellings Act of 1909 authorized loans for home building. In South Australia an Advances for Homes Act of 1910 established a fund which lent up to 80 per cent of the value of land and improvements; and in Victoria a Land Purchase and Management Board was empowered to acquire private lands for subdivision and improvement, to dispose of them in allotments not exceeding $1,200 in value, and to erect dwellings valued at a similar figure.[13]

The MHC did not intend immediate, literal adoption of the New Zealand and Australian policies. It proposed, rather, an "experiment" to demonstrate whether or not "wholesome dwellings" could be erected within the means of low-paid workers, and hoped that a successful experiment, proving that "there is a reasonable profit in the construction of such homes," would encourage private capital to enter the field.[14] The constitutional amendment of 1915 and the legislative appropriation of $50,000 in 1917 enabled the Commission to undertake its demonstration.

The intensive consideration given to problems of design, sub-division, and site-planning, the use of state capital, and the conception of the project as the first episode in a broader scheme of urban decentralization and population regrouping combined to make the Lowell experiment unique for its time. Even before receiving its appropriation, the Commission began examing plans and models of low-cost workers housing. It discovered satisfactory Massachusetts precedents in Billerica, where a limited-dividend "garden suburb" company produced a "semi-bungalow" for approximately $1,800, and in Salem, where a "Rebuilding Trust" organized after the devastating fire of 1912 erected semi-detached brick homes costing $1,791 apiece. The Commission was impressed also by the six-room, $1,600 houses in Kistler, Pennsylvania, built by the Mount Union Refractories Company, as well as the projected single-family detached homes of the Kenosha (Wisconsin) Homes Company, costing $1,800 to $2,000. Rarely had so much thought been applied to the structure, quality, and social purpose of low-cost housing. As criteria for its own homes, the Commission specified a living room, kitchen, three bedrooms, cellar, and adequate facilities for cooking, heating, lighting, washing, and waste disposal. The subdivision plans of the Commission provided for a low density of eight families per acre and lot dimensions of 40 x 100 feet. The house was to occupy only 40 feet of the lot depth, leaving 10 feet for a front yard and 50 feet for a garden. Regarding the "proper and profitable use" of the garden as central to its entire scheme, the Commission hired a garden expert on a part-time basis to provide "competent instruction and supervision." It anticipated that families could increase their incomes by $36 a year (or reduce their rent by $3 a month) from vegetable and poultry products.

Although the Commission had originally hoped for a $100,000 appropriation, intending to construct some fifty homesteads at $2,000, it received only half that sum. This reduction, combined with a steep rise in prices when the Commission was ready to begin construction in October 1917, cut the project to twelve homesteads at a minimum cost per house of $2,400. Its choice of a seven-acre plot along Hildreth Street in Lowell was based upon careful consideration of site and locational advantages.[15] Soil experts from the Massachusetts Agricultural College certified to the suitability of the land for gardening. The tract was close to Merrimack Square, the business center of Lowell, and to the mills across the Merrimack River. A public and parochial school adjoined the development, which included eight five-room detached and two four-room semi-detached cottages. Of frame construction, the dwellings ranged in cost from $2,400 to $3,100 and were intended for workers earning $14 a week or less. Arthur Comey, a Cambridge, Massachusetts, landscape architect and a member of the Commission, prepared the subdivision plan and assisted in designing the cottages.

The MHC received no additional appropriations to continue its housing experiment. Abolished in 1919, its functions were transferred to the Department of Public Welfare, which provided an agent in Lowell to collect installments, supervise the property, and instruct purchasers in gardening. In its efforts to discover the underlying principles of good housing environment through innovations in financing, design and site-planning, and broadly-conceived planning objectives, the MHC transcended in significance the little community of twelve homes in Lowell.

Chapter 2

THE UNITED STATES had entered World War I several months before the MHC began construction at Lowell. A serious housing shortage developed, particularly in armaments and ship-building centers, forcing the federal government to engage in housing operations which quickly overshadowed those of the MHC. Acting through the Emergency Fleet Corporation of the U. S. Shipping Board, and the U. S. Housing Corporation, the government built or supervised the construction of several thousand dwellings for war workers and their families. The standards of community planning achieved through the war housing inspired a generation of architects and planners who hoped that similar standards might be applied in peacetime.[1] War housing also encouraged the belief that government help was necessary for any long-range solution to the housing crisis which erupted following the armistice.

This crisis, reaching its peak between 1919 and 1921, marked a turning point in American housing development. The collapse of the building industry, the nation-wide housing shortage, the rapid rise in

17

housing costs and rentals, the low vacancy levels, all combined to discredit restrictive legislation as the key to housing betterment. The worst of the housing emergency was over by 1922, but it had launched a continuing search for alternatives to restrictive legislation through which low-, and middle-income groups could be assured a sufficient supply of good housing at costs or rentals which they could afford.

Unlike European nations, which had long supplemented housing codes with constructive measures including public housing, municipal land purchase, low-interest loans to individuals and limited-dividend companies, and tax exemptions, the United States was thoroughly unequipped to deal with its postwar housing dilemma. It lacked any governmental machinery to compensate for the collapse of the private building industry, which had assumed exclusive responsibility for satisfying the nation's housing needs. Before the 1920's the small-scale, speculative builder did meet, for better or worse, the shelter needs of the urban population. Low-income housing was profitable, and although the wooden triple-decker of New England, the dumb-bell tenement of New York, and the tightly packed row-houses of Philadelphia were discredited as higher standards evolved, they at least provided shelter for groups unable to command a superior product in the open market. The exponents of constructive housing legislation in the 1920's responded to a situation created by the withdrawal of the speculative builder from the low- and even middle-income housing market.

The anticipated resumption of normal building operations following the armistice in the fall of 1918 did not materialize. Lack of capital for residential building and inflationary construction costs discouraged commercial builders from resuming their ante-bellum activities, despite abnormal scarcity and demand. Unable to compete with industrial and commercial demand for labor, supplies, and capital, residential construction benefited least from the building boom which lasted from the spring of 1919 to the spring of 1920. Construction costs climbed far above their prewar level during this period. The all-commodity wholesale price index increased 29 per cent between April 1919 and April 1920, but wholesale building material prices rose 72 per cent. Union wage scales advanced by at least 35 per cent. Sensitive to rising costs, residential construction declined sharply after a short spurt early in 1919. Building volume picked up in 1921, the number of nonfarm dwelling unit starts reaching 449,000 and rising to 716,000 in 1922. For the entire decade, the average number of units started was in the 700,000 vicinity, a total not reached until four years after the conclusion of the War.

Rising rents paralleled the shortage of new construction. Advancing moderately during the first half of 1919, rents increased by 18 per cent between June 1919 and June 1920, when they stood at 29 per cent above the prewar level. The speculative purchase of homes and apartments and their resale at prices based on new rent schedules contributed to the rent rise. According to a survey of 178 cities conducted by the National Industrial Conference Board, rents rose 85 per cent between July 1914 and June 1924.

Price inflation reached its peak in the spring of 1920, but building costs remained at a permanently high plateau throughout the 1920's. Even though wholesale building material prices declined some 40 per cent by the spring of 1922 from their peak in the spring of 1920 they remained, at their lowest point, 72 per cent higher than the prewar level. Prices rose again in 1923 and for the rest of the decade remained 80 to 100 per cent higher than in the prewar period.[2]

Housing reformers of the Progressive era had protested against the quality of housing erected by commercial builders for low-income groups, and had labored to raise standards by means of restrictive legislation. They never confronted the desperate shortage which characterized the four postwar years. Any housing program based upon restrictive legislation, which could only raise costs further but could not produce new housing, was pointless. The scarcity generated a nation-wide chorus of protest and dismay. Speaking for the Philadelphia Chapter of the American Institute of Architects, John Irwin Bright complained that "with housing standing in the first group of civilization's demands, the terrible indictment lies against the industrial system that throughout the entire world it is impossible to build a home for those earning low wages or salaries at a cost which will allow it to be rented or sold without a loss." "From every section of the State of California," according to the California Commission of Immigration and Housing, "comes the cry for more houses —more housing accommodation—and the remedies suggested vary from tent cities and the use of public buildings to the closing of the doors of the state to transient population." The Commission added that the "problem daily becomes more and more serious, as the present building program of the state is not even meeting the normal required housing increase, to say nothing of making up the shortage, which developed during the war period." In Pennsylvania, observed the director of the Chamber of Commerce Housing Bureau in 1920, the "shortage of homes has reached such stupendous proportions that what was formerly a social question . . . has come to be a real live economic problem—an industrial menace." The housing committee of the New York State Association of Architects reported in the same year that the "machinery of speculative and competitive enterprise for the production of houses has broken down." "At the present time," according to the Committee, "it does not pay to build even the kind of house that the speculative builder formerly supplied the moderately well-to-do." And in the spring of 1919 the City and Suburban Homes Company, a large model-housing organization, described the rent question in New York as a "burning one." "The production of houses has been far below the normal for three years as a result of war causes," the Company complained, "and with the present high construction costs, it is hardly probable that new building can be expected through the ordinary agencies." [3]

Despite the upswing in housing production by 1922, the executive secretary of the Better Housing League of Cincinnati maintained that "not for decades has the housing problem been so acute as during the past two or three years. For almost the first time in recent history it has ceased to be a problem for the submerged tenth alone, and has hit squarely the people of moderate means." [4] And in Philadelphia the secretary of the Philadelphia Housing Association announced in 1921 that a "nation-wide housing problem confronts the United States." Following a survey of fourteen industrial districts covering 70,832 dwelling units, the Association discovered only eighty-three houses renting for $50 or less a month that were vacant, available, and fit for occupancy. If the rental limit was set at $30, the number of vacancies dropped to fifty-eight. Rents between 1914 and 1921 had risen from $14.20 to $20.90 a month, an increase of almost 50 per cent. Permits for new houses, which had reached 5,307 in 1919, dropped in 1920 to 1,306. The Association estimated that the housing under construction in the first half of 1921 totaled only 13 per cent of the minimum yearly need. [5]

Before America's entry into the war, constructive housing legislation was limited to a 1915 Oklahoma law authorizing the Commissioners of the Land Office to loan money to individuals or families for homes. As never before in American history the postwar housing crisis, following closely upon the federal housing experiment, focused attention upon the role of government in housing and stimulated a flock of proposals for direct government assistance. A Milwaukee Housing Commission, appointed by socialist Mayor Hoan, endorsed the work of the MHC and condemned the speculative building methods which "have failed in Europe and in this country to provide wage earners' homes of a type commensurate with the cost involved." [6] The

Commission recommended municipal land ownership to eliminate the burden of speculative incre-
ments and a program of "constructive legislation
stimulating the erection of wholesome homes for
wage earners through state or municipal loans." As
a result of these recommendations, a state enabling
act was passed which authorized cities and counties
to purchase stock in cooperative housing companies.
A Garden Homes Company was then organized in
1920. The City and County of Milwaukee subscribed
to the stock of the Company, which erected 105
homes.

Most of the postwar proposals for constructive
housing legislation failed. In North Dakota, for example, a Home Building Association operated by
the State Industrial Commission was established in
1919 and authorized to construct, repair, or remodel
buildings for sale at a price not exceeding $5,000.
Nothing was accomplished. Equally unproductive
was a State Housing Committee appointed in Louisiana in 1918 to obtain federal aid for housing.
The Pittsburgh City Council prepared a bill authorizing municipal building operations, but it died
in committee. In Boston an unsuccessful bill was
drawn up which permitted the city to acquire land
and build homes, and in Paterson, New Jersey, the
mayor appointed a committee which futilely recommended an expenditure of one-and-a-half-million dollars for housing. More successful than most was
the small city of Cohoes, New York. It had ap-
propriated some $100,000 for housing during the
War, and in 1924 the mayor reported that the city
had taken an option on thirty acres of land which it

proposed to "develop [into] a community with ideal arrangements." [7]

The California Veterans' Farm and Home Purchase Act of 1921 represented the most ambitious and successful program of constructive housing legislation to emerge in the immediate postwar period. It was actually the state's second housing venture. Back in 1915 the legislature had appointed a Commission on Land Colonization and Rural Credits whose chairman, Elwood Mead, was an engineer long associated with the conservation movement and an international authority on irrigation. He had recently returned from an eight-year stay in Victoria (Australia), where he had served as chairman of the State Rivers and Water Supply Commission. Under Mead's direction, the California Commission prepared a report which deplored the disappearance of good public land, the rising prices of private farm land, the spread of tenant farming, and the "increasing attractions of city life which threaten the social impairment of rural communities." [8] It recommended the development of a systematic state land settlement or colonization policy, and in 1917 a Land Settlement Act authorized the appointment of a Land Settlement Board which sponsored two separate farm communities. One of these, Durham Land Settlement (in Butte County north of Sacramento), contained 6,200 acres subdivided into tracts of 20 to 160 acres, with various community facilities such as a school, a church, and a community hall. The Delhi Settlement (San Joaquin Valley south of Sacramento) contained 8,700 acres of desert land dependent upon irrigation.

It accommodated over 200 families. The California Farm and Home Purchase Act of 1921 represented, in part, a continuation of the "back-to-the-soil" policy personified in the Land Settlement Act, but without the communitarian features. It provided for state purchase or construction of farms or homes and gardens to be sold to veterans on liberal credit terms. By 1928, the state had invested twenty-four million dollars in the project, involving the erection or purchase of nearly 5,000 homes and 250 farms.[9]

The various proposals for the use of government capital or credit between 1918 and 1922 signified a response to a severe housing shortage caused by price inflation and the withdrawal of speculative capital. As a New York architect explained the situation: "Owing to the great increase in cost of building construction about twice the amount of capital is now needed in order to put through a housing operation. In the face of this increased requirement, there is less capital for building than before the war. Investors have withdrawn capital from real estate, because they fear the risk of building under the uncertain conditions of the day, and because they can obtain a higher return on well-secured stocks and bonds." [10]

Even the return of speculative capital to residential construction by 1922 did not impress the housing economist Edith Elmer Wood. Building and lending agencies, she argued, could no longer profitably supply the housing needs of low- and middle-income groups. A permanent "economic *impasse*" had emerged in the 1920's rooted in a scarcity of low-interest capital. "The crux of the situation which confronts us," Mrs. Wood maintained, "is the excessive cost of home-building." In her opinion, "many have come to feel in this country, as students of housing did in the older countries years ago, that the only source which commands a sufficient supply of credit and can provide it economically at a sufficiently low rate of interest is the Government." [11] The inadequacies of commercial housing finance became Mrs. Wood's *idée fixe,* and she persisted throughout the 1920's in a vigorous campaign to establish an economic rationale for the use of government capital in housing. Possessing an encyclopedic knowledge of foreign aid-to-housing programs, and impressed particularly with the achievements of England, Belgium, and Germany, she emphasized that these three nations had "made the supply of credit at a low rate of interest the keystone of their system." [12] She then outlined for this country a program which hinged on the supply of credit by federal, state, and local agencies for the benefit of the two-thirds of the population whose incomes totaled $2,000 or less.

Mrs. Wood had actually launched her crusade for constructive housing legislation long before World War I, and thus ranks as one of the earliest rebels against the restrictive legislation program of the Progressive era inspired and led by Lawrence Veiller of New York. President Roosevelt's Homes Commission of Washington, D. C., had recommended in 1908 that Congress authorize low-interest loans to limited-dividend building associations, but nothing happened until 1913 when Mrs. Wood prepared a bill introduced into Congress by Repsentative Borland of Missouri and Senator Pomerene of Ohio. Neither this bill, nor a revised version in 1916 (which not only provided for loans to limited-dividend companies, but also permitted the commissioners of the District to build homes and lend money to individuals for the purpose), was enacted.

In the 1920's Mrs. Wood labored to secure acceptance of a government aid-to-housing program which she had worked out fairly completely by 1919. It included the establishment of a National Housing Commission equipped to loan funds to local communities and limited-dividend companies for housing projects approved by her proposed state housing and town planning commissions. Also on the federal level, she advised amendment of the Federal Reserve Act to permit national banks to supply housing loans, and amendment of the Farm Loan Act for the same purpose. One of her favorite proposals involved the use of postal savings deposits for housing loans to individuals. Abortive bills authorizing such loans had been introduced into the House of Representatives in 1913 and 1915. On the state level, Mrs. Wood envisioned the creation of housing and town planning commissions to approve applications for loans from the National Housing Commission and to supply its own loans drawn from a state housing fund. Finally, Mrs. Wood proposed local housing and town planning boards whose responsibilities included encouragement of limited-dividend and cooperative housing and formulation of a municipal housing program which might or might not include public housing.[13]

Fully acquainted with the work of the MHC, Mrs. Wood's own thinking was probably influenced by its stress upon the need for low-interest capital and local planning agencies especially devoted to housing betterment. Clarence S. Stein, a New York architect and another leading exponent of government housing credit in the 1920's, had not been aware of the Massachusetts group, even though he and his associates in the RPAA evolved a philosophy and a program similar in many essentials—but bolder and more comprehensive. Instead of a single experiment designed to prove that cheap but satisfactory homes could be erected for workers, thus serving as an object lesson to private enterprise, Stein concluded, like Mrs. Wood, that the inability of commercial builders and lenders to satisfy the housing needs of low- and middle-income groups necessitated a long-range program of government aid. The supply and cost of capital, however, represented only one factor in housing costs, and the RPAA devoted considerable attention to analyzing all the elements which influenced housing supply and quality.

The MHC, in sharp contrast to the average speculative developer, had carefully analyzed the design and location of its Lowell homesteads, recognizing that in group or community housing developments combined with intelligent site-planning lay untapped possibilities for economy and amenity. In its modest way, the Commission pointed the way towards the greater achievements of the federal World War I housing program and those of Stein and Henry Wright at Sunnyside and Radburn.

Sunnyside and Radburn were originally conceived as small beginnings in what the RPAA hoped would result in a full-scale urban reorganization and social reconstruction within the framework of the regional city. The MHC anticipated the regionalism of the RPAA when it called for urban decentralization and an urban-rural equilibrium, when it criticized the adverse effects of urban congestion, and when it complained of the social and physical debilitation of the countryside. The RPAA, however, went far beyond the MHC in its elaboration of the philosophic and technological foundations of regionalism; for although the RPAA's regionalism and community planning synthesis were inspired in part by a romantic idealization of the rural, it never succumbed to the naive Jeffersonian agrarianism characteristic of the MHC.

Chapter 3

T HE ORIGINS OF the RPAA are traceable, in
some degree, to the postwar housing crisis, a
dramatic episode which confirmed to Stein, Mumford, and others in the group the necessity of sub-
stituting in place of the speculative city-building
of the past a community planning method which
"considers the physical changes in due relation to
the social situation of which they are a part." [1] One
finds Mumford complaining as early as 1919 of the
constriction of city planning "within the present
tangle of private property interests," and aspiring
toward a "unified scheme of regional development." [2]
That same year Governor Alfred Smith of New
York appointed a Reconstruction Commission; and
when Clarence Stein volunteered his services as
secretary of its Housing Committee, he launched
the sequence of events leading to the establishment
of the RPAA and the New York State Commission
of Housing and Regional Planning in 1923, the
City Housing Corporation in 1924, and the New
York Housing Law of 1926. Mumford described
him as the "most dynamic member of our group"

31

and the "decisive leader of the whole movement from 1922 on." [3]

Stein was born in Rochester, New York, in 1882. Following a trip to Europe in 1902, he enrolled in the Columbia School of Architecture intending to become an interior decorator. Dissatisfied after one year's exposure to the classic curriculum at Columbia, he left for Paris and work in a decorator's studio. Deciding, however, to become an architect, Stein entered the École des Beaux-Arts. He remained in Europe until 1911, when he returned to the United States and entered the office of Bertram G. Goodhue. Stein remained with Goodhue for seven years, and during that time worked on such projects as St. Bartholomew's Church in New York, the San Diego World's Fair, and the Village of Tyrone, New Mexico, sponsored by the Phelps Dodge Company. After serving a year as a First Lieutenant in the Engineers, he set up an independent practice in 1919.

Stein had been secretary from 1915 to 1919 of the City Planning Committee of the City Club, a civic betterment organization, but his affiliation with the Hudson Guild in 1919 proved more influential in directing his attention to social architecture. A West Side social settlement, the Guild linked Stein with the problems of New York's poor, and its director, John Lovejoy Elliott, exerted an "inspiring" personal influence. As chairman of the Hudson Guild Farm Committee, Stein spent many weekends at the Netcong, New Jersey, farm, whose dining hall he designed in 1920. From 1923 to 1926 the RPAA held occasional weekend meetings at the farm,[4] and often used the City Club in New York for luncheons.

Throughout the 1920's, Stein maintains, he and Henry Wright viewed their central challenge as how to promote good housing and communities at minimum cost. Believing that the problem was not simply better residential environments but also making them accessible to low-income groups, the question of money necessarily pervaded the thinking of the RPAA.[5] Thus Mumford describes the major change effected by the RPAA as a "fresh vision of what, on sound economic terms, a good urban community might be."[6] As secretary of the Housing Committee of the Reconstruction Commission, Stein examined this money and cost problem at an early date. The Committee's conclusions shaped his thinking for years to come.

In its report of March 1920, the Committee adopted as its basic premise the fact that "it is economically unprofitable now, it has been economically impossible for many years past to provide a large part of the population of this State with decent homes according to American standards of living. Decent homes and wholesome environments in which to bring up children cost more than most workers can afford."[7] Estimating that New York required 40,000 new dwelling units, the Committee emphasized not only that new construction had virtually ceased, but that it had declined steadily since 1915. In that year 1,365 new-law tenements were erected, dropping to 1,207 in 1916, 760 in 1917, 130 in 1918, and 89 in 1919. The overall tenement vacancy rate had declined from 5.6 per cent in the spring of 1916 to 2.18 in 1919 (and only .06 in new-law tenements). Even the few new-law tenements undergoing construction, the Committee complained, were beyond the range of most workers because the "price of construction has risen so high and the uncertainty as to cost is so great that it is necessary to charge for new construction a rental far beyond the means of a large part of our population." [8]

The Committee's analysis of the housing problem and the conclusions reached differed sharply from the typical housing survey of the Progressive era. The prewar survey tended to focus upon the sanitary and social pathology of the slums, supplemented by recommendations for code enactment and enforcement; but in 1919–1920 minimum standards legislation to control commercial builders had no relevance to the existing situation, and Stein's Committee directed its attention instead to means by which to increase the supply and reduce the cost of housing.

The specific, and for the time, radical, recommendations of the Committee majority to the legislature included establishment of a central state housing agency and local housing boards in communities of 10,000 or more population, enactment of a constitutional amendment permitting state housing credit, and an enabling act authorizing cities to acquire land and, if necessary, engage in housing operations.

It further urged municipal ownership of land to eliminate the waste inherent in speculative withdrawal, trading or premature subdivision. The Committee objected vehemently to the practice of land subdivision long in advance of settlement, and to inefficient, standardized street-platting, both of which raised housing costs unnecessarily. For purposes of additional economy, it favored "large scale operation in the building of houses" in contrast to the scattered "building of small individual units." Turning to broader issues, the Committee asserted that housing could not be separated from industrial or transportation policy, and therefore "we must recognize that the solution of the housing problem means community planning in a large sense." Eying the English Garden City, it linked housing improvement to industrial decentralization and limitations upon the size of cities. The Committee, finally, observed that a "policy of loaning money at low interest rates for housing has been developed by almost every other civilized country, excepting America." [9]

Ignoring the Committee's recommendations, despite Governor Smith's firm support, the legislature instead passed a rent control measure at its regular session in the spring of 1920, supplementing this with a tax exemption law at a special session in the fall.[10] The tax measure, which incorporated no controls whatever over standards or rentals, was simply a subsidy to the building industry. It permitted local communities to exempt all new dwellings except hotels from taxation until 1932, if construction began before April 1, 1922, and was completed within two years. The exemption was limited to $5,000 for a single-family house, $10,000 for a two-family house, and $1,000 per room (with a maximum of $5,000 per family dwelling unit) for apartment houses. New York City alone took advantage of the tax exemption law, enacting the necessary legislation in February 1921.

Tax exemption broke the building deadlock in New York, but since it involved no limitations upon rentals, and since rent controls did not apply to new construction, it contributed little to the low-cost housing supply. The New York State Commission of Housing and Regional Planning (CHRP) found in 1923 that rents in few instances fell below $15 per room per month in the new apartments, or $45 for a three-room unit. Assuming that a family could not comfortably expend more than 20 per cent of its income for rent, the Commission maintained that the new construction was beyond the reach of the 69 per cent of New York families whose incomes did not exceed $2,500 a year.[11] Indeed, rents climbed steeply in the three years following enactment of tax exemption. Using December 1914 as a base, U. S. Bureau of Labor Statistics figures showed that rents which stood at 138.1 in December 1920 had soared to 162.4 by December 1923. They continued to rise during the decade, but at a slower pace, reaching 170.2 in December 1926. New York's postwar housing experience was not unique. In several major cities rents rose even more sharply. They had almost doubled for example in Chicago and Detroit between 1914 and 1926, and increased more steeply in Buffalo, Philadelphia, Cleveland, and Baltimore than in New York.[12]

The building revival in New York beginning in 1921 under the auspices of the tax exemption law not only failed to benefit lower-income groups, but hardly kept pace with effective demand. The net increase in dwelling units, which rose steadily from 10,708 in 1921 to 90,691 in 1924 barely affected overall vacancy levels. A vacancy rate of 2.18 in March 1919 declined to .36 in April 1920 and reached a nadir of .15 in February 1921. It then climbed slowly to .37 in March 1923 and .80 in January 1924, but did not reach the "safe" 5 per cent margin until January 1927—more than eight years after the conclusion of the War. The housing situation was even more serious than the crude vacancy percentages indicate; vacancies were generally lowest for the better new-law tenements built after 1901, suggesting that poorer families resorted to any kind of accommodation to find shelter. The housing shortage apparently provided many old-law tenements with a stay of execution. Vacancy rates for old-law tenements dropped from 4.90 in March 1917 to .16 in February 1921 and remained at less than 1 per cent until 1925.[13]

The postwar housing crisis—compounded of shortage, price inflation, rising rentals, and a scarcity of capital—was real enough; but neither it nor the subsequent building revival, which witnessed a sharp increase in costs and rentals, can fully explain the views and the program of the RPAA. One cannot understand their argument that the commercial builder was incapable of supplying the housing needs of the majority of families in the 1920's (and had never satisfied those of the lowest-income groups) unless one considers the qualitative norms which always affected their judgment of the housing situation. It was not the literal shortage of shelter, particularly by the mid-1920's, that explains the RPAA's position, but tenaciously held social and community values. Stein, for example, complained in 1924 that "away out toward Coney Island there is feverish construction—little rows of ugly, badly built wooden structures." This kind of commercial development convinced him that "even the housing which is constructed by speculative builders does not meet the needs of the people for a healthy and sane community life. The urge for profit demands the use of every bit of space legally available." In a similar vein, Mumford stigmatized the offering of the commercial builder:

Given an income of $2,400 or $3,000 a year, what can a family get for it under present conditions in and around our great cities? Precious little. Semi-detached houses whose surrounding open spaces are covered by a multitude of auto drives and garages—that is Flatbush. Rows of mean little single-family houses, backed by wretched little drying-greens and alleys—that is West Philadelphia and Long Island City. Three, four and five-story apartment houses with every modern improvement, but lacking in sunlight, fresh air, beauty, freedom from noise and privacy—that is Boston, Chicago, and the Bronx. These are not permanent homes for women and children; they are dormitory slums.[14]

The RPAA hoped to provide alternatives on a satisfactory economic basis to what Stein and Mumford described. Several of its charter members also belonged to the Committee on Community Planning of the American Institute of Architects. The RPAA was established to help carry out the community planning program formulated by the CCP-AIA, but the new organization introduced a more explicit regional content. It proposed to "assist as far as it can in contracting the present haphazard growth of cities in America. This it believes can only be done by deliberately planning whole regions. . . . It proposes to further its objects not only by the study of housing, industrial decentralization, city planning and regional planning, but also by aiding in the formation of associations and corporations, designed to plan and build garden cities." [15]

Stein assumed the chairmanship of the CCP-AIA in 1921 and was succeeded by Henry Wright in 1925.[16] Although more limited in scope and membership, the Committee paralleled the RPAA throughout the 1920's in promoting a community planning program. The CCP-AIA outlined its views in the pages of the *Journal of the American Institute of Architects,* edited by Charles Harris Whitaker, whom Stein regarded as "an inspiring person and a great editor." [17] Whitaker was a single-taxer contemptuous of the prewar efforts to improve housing conditions through restrictive legislation. He had sent Frederick L. Ackerman to England in 1915 to report on British war housing. Impressed with the fact that the British were building permanent homes in communities planned along Garden City lines, he exerted every influence to insure that American war housing approximated the British policy of permanent community building. The Emergency Fleet Corporation and the U. S. Housing Corporation became training schools in community planning, providing experience in large-scale design and site-planning for future charter members of the RPAA like Robert D. Kohn, Ackerman, and Wright. As a consequence, war housing, according to Mumford, "gave a fresh incentive to the housing movement, and pushed it along paths that the older housing reformers never envisaged." [18]

After the War, Whitaker played an important role in bringing together the men who later formed the RPAA.[19] This he accomplished by opening the pages of the *Journal* to their commentary and by personal introduction. Stein, for example, first met Benton MacKaye in the summer of 1921 when Whitaker introduced them at the Hudson Guild Farm.[20] Besides Stein, Wright, Mumford, MacKaye, Whitaker, and Ackerman, charter members included Stuart Chase (economist), Alexander Bing (realtor), Robert D. Kohn (architect), John Irwin Bright (architect), and Frederick Bigger (architect). Others associated with the group during the decade of its existence included Edith Elmer Wood, Tracy Augur, Catherine Bauer, Robert Bruère, Joseph K. Hart, and Clarence Perry. Ackerman belonged to the small inner circle, as did Catherine Bauer towards the end.[21] Although he was the original catalyst, Whitaker eventually dropped out of the RPAA for personal and ideological reasons.

In one sense, the RPAA was an informal school for training and education in community planning. It often invited individuals prominent in urban affairs and welfare to its sessions in New York or at the Hudson Guild Farm, hoping to benefit from their suggestions and criticisms. The fact that men like John Lovejoy Elliott, Clarence Perry, and Geddes Smith participated in its deliberations helped link the RPAA with the social work community of New York.[22] A casual operation, with no elections, permanent executive secretary, or mailing list, it never included more than twenty members. Its size and informality were deliberate. "By keeping away from 'organization,'" Mumford explains, "the RPAA proved the value of 'association.'"[23] It is perhaps misleading even to refer to the RPAA in any collective sense. Unstructured and unconcerned with achieving consensus expressed in official policy statements, its strength lay, according to Mumford, "in the looseness and flexibility of our relationships, in our respect for each other's individuality, with all our differences overcome and bonded together by our friendship, and our very close association, for long periods almost daily."[24]

The influence and practical achievements of the RPAA were largely the product of an inner circle, which pooled together an impressive array of complementary talents. Along with a youthful, somewhat impatient zeal, Mumford possessed an interest in history, a knack for architectural and social criticism, and a compelling literary style through which the RPAA transmitted its message. He imported the concept of regionalism into this country and insured its incorporation into the thinking of the group. Having been attracted by the progressive housing policies outlined in the *Journal of the American Institute of Architects* around 1917, his affiliation with those who later formed the RPAA began in the fall of 1919, when he met Whitaker in Washington, D. C. The latter introduced him to both Stein and MacKaye.[25]

An experienced forester, disciple of Thoreau, and ardent naturalist, MacKaye helped translate the regional ideal into working programs. Henry Wright, a native of St. Louis and son of an accountant, possessed a keen talent for economic analysis which he applied to demonstrating how interest rates and technological improvement affected housing costs. Stein compared his intuitive grasp of site-planning to that of Raymond Unwin.[26] Stein himself excelled as a promoter. His cordial and relaxed manner concealed a tough determination to translate ideas into action, and he linked the group to the Al Smith regime. Finding Smith personally interested in housing and open to suggestion, Stein labored to convince the Governor of the need for direct state aid.[27]

The relationship of Frederick Ackerman, a brilliant architectural technician, to the inner circle was ambiguous. A worshipper of Veblen, and an incorrigible skeptic, he is described by Mumford as the "advocatus diaboli for Stein's and Wright's constructive ideas; something of a wet blanket, but never outside the group." [28] Applying an austere Veblenian analysis to American social and economic institutions, Ackerman was dubious of the prospects for community planning in the absence of a fundamental reconstruction of those institutions and the values they embodied. Interested in the role of the technician in modern life, but convinced that the "instinct of workmanship" and speculative capitalism were incompatible, Ackerman believed that neither the architectural technician nor any other specialist could apply his skill for maximum social advantage as long as individuals were able to capitalize technological gain in terms of price. He interpreted urban growth, past and present, as largely a response to pecuniary imperatives; efficient and socially productive land use had been subordinated to speculative gain. Ackerman thus viewed the nuclear problem for the social architect and planner as transference of urban development from the "sphere of the interplay of self-regarding actions into the province of social design and control." [29]

Ackerman carried to an extreme an anti-speculative bias which pervaded every feature of the RPAA's program. One can interpret its community planning synthesis, in part, as an effort to create a new institutional framework through which the social architect and planner formulated urban physical and social goals. In their criticism of speculative business interests, particularly banking and real estate agencies, and the technicians who uncomplainingly acquiesced in the institutional framework which those interests provided, the members of the RPAA personified the idea of an administered society. The historic conflict, in their eyes, lay between the tradition of pioneer waste, resource exploitation, and individual aggrandizement, on the one hand, administered communal growth, social controls, and efficient land classification and use, on the other. Obstinate in their refusal to equate community progress with physical growth and rising property values, members of the RPAA expounded their views with little regard for their reputation as "realists." In Mumford's words, "When one wishes to get a new idea accepted one concentrates on that idea: one is under no obligation, if one hopes for acceptance and action, to dwell exhaustively upon

the complexities of the task, and to accept in advance
all the modifications and compromises that will
have to be made before the idea will prove viable
in practice." [30] It was this strategy which helps
explain the frequent citation to the Garden City:
neither an ideal form nor an exclusive goal, it was
a starting point for action.

The new institutional framework for city-
building, enlarging the role of the architect, planner,
and welfare expert in determining urban physical
structure and social organization, was outlined in a
1925 report of the CCP-AIA. Prepared by Mumford
from materials supplied by the Committee,[31] this
document is significant for its sweeping historical
criticism of traditional speculative development and
delineation of new architectural, housing, and
planning policy. Complaining that cities ruthlessly
sacrificed residential needs to those of real estate
speculators, traffic, and commerce, a trend already
apparent by the end of the eighteenth century, the
Committee interpreted the contemporary city as an
inheritance largely of the pioneer ethos. Thus the
rectangular block, "planned in advance of use and
without reference to use," as in the Plan of the
Commissioners for Manhattan Island in 1811,
was a kind of pseudo-planning responding primarily
to commercial imperatives. It often made no sense
in terms of topography, residential amenity and
convenience, or the ultimate use to which the land
was put. Subdivided, however, into deep, narrow,
standardized lots, the rectangular block had served
all too well the needs of a pioneer society, and the
speculator and trader in land: "The swiftness with

which the rectangular plan could be laid out by the least imaginative of surveyors, the equal ease with which each block could be subdivided, lent itself to the haste of the pioneer." The effects of this mechanical pseudo-planning, however, were disastrous for housing, resulting in "dark interior rooms, wasteful corridors, and a tendency to build over areas that should be used for courts and gardens." Such specimens as the railroad and dumb-bell tenements of New York and the "depressing" row houses of Philadelphia were in reality "planned to fit the requirements of lots rather than to serve the uses of the tenants." [32]

The Committee interpreted the city planning movement as it had evolved since the 1890's as little more than an effort to apply palliatives which ignored fundamental questions of urban purpose and structure. It dismissed the City Beautiful, inspired by the Chicago Fair of 1893, as "an attempt to put a pleasing front upon the scrappy building, upon the monotonous streets and the mean houses, that characterized the larger American cities." The City Beautiful was soon succeeded by a utilitarian planning in which experts and technicians, heralding the arrival of a new profession, applied themselves diligently to superficialities which increased land values and congestion. Obsessed with the "bare physical framework of the city," they concentrated upon zoning, street-widening, rapid transit facilities, and other engineering feats, omitting from their calculations the "whole environment, including the work, the housing, the recreation, the customs and habits of the people who make up a community." No amount of zoning, however, which stabilized land values at a high level, or uncoordinated transit and utility improvements which made it possible for more people to enter and live in the central city, could substitute for a satisfactory answer to the question upon which depended the ultimate quality of urban life: "How big must a city be to perform effectively all of its social, educational, and industrial functions?" [33]

The Committee proposed a clear-cut alternative to unlimited metropolitan expansion, which it charged was responsible for the inflated land values and congestion which lowered housing standards and necessitated enormous expenditure for transit systems and utilities, thus diverting valuable funds from cultural and educational facilities. It favored the "comprehensive and enlightened group action necessary to create the Garden City, and to create that new regional framework, based upon the more effective relation of communities and industries to the natural environment, to power, to water, to fresh air and 'nature,' in which garden cities will be possible." [34]

The architect, the Committee insisted, had a vested interest in promoting community planning, for in no other way could he control the factors which determined the ultimate quality of his work. As things stood, the transit official, engineer, realtor, and sanitarian formulated the legal codes and physical skeleton in which the individual building had to fit, thus forcing the architect and client to "work within the rigid frame that these special interests have . . . provided." Confronted with a standardized street and subdivision plan, and forced to crowd the land where congestion was great and land values high, the architect controlled neither the building nor its relationship to the site. Equally important, "one of the outstanding elements in cost"— the rate of money—was "outside the province of both the architect and the community planner," a fact which diminished the possibility of providing good low-cost housing. Finally, the architect needed the Garden City and similar community developments to supply opportunities to design those large-scale group projects through which he could exercise his creative talents and supply the best housing at the least cost. On the grounds of both economy and amenity the Committee objected to the unending miles of detached and semi-detached flats and homes which spanned the American city. These offered "neither privacy nor comfort nor free exposure to air and sunlight," and the Committee contrasted them to the row houses planned as units and correlated with the street and utility system which had been produced by the federal war housing agencies.[35]

The kernel of the RPAA's program was the co-operation of the social architect and planner in the design of large-scale group and community housing, financed in some measure by low-interest government loans, and directed toward the creation of the regional city. Sunnyside and Radburn were conceived as first steps in its realization. Contrary to the expectations or at least the hopes of the RPAA, they did not restrain the tide of metropolitan expansion or transform the regional city from an idea to a controlling factor in American urban development. Sunnyside and Radburn did represent a practical application of large-scale social architecture as conceived by the RPAA, and they demonstrated one approach to the planning of residential environments which accommodated the full range of needs of a twentieth-century urban population.

Chapter 4

R AYMOND UNWIN exerted the greatest single influence in shaping the RPAA's thinking on
the economics and site-planning of residential neighborhoods. Stein and Wright journeyed to England in
1924, the year Sunnyside was begun, in order to
examine intensively the garden cities and suburbs
which Unwin had helped design, and while there
visited him and Ebenezer Howard.[1] The two American architects were familiar with Unwin's *Nothing Gained by Overcrowding,* a pamphlet first published in 1912, which proved to their satisfaction
that lower building densities yielded as much to the
investor as higher densities. The economic waste
represented by streets was the key to Unwin's analysis. Streets were both the most expensive and least
satisfactory form of open space imaginable. But the
fewer the houses, the fewer the streets needed to provide frontage and, conversely, the fewer the streets
the more land available for each house and the
greater the surplus of land for recreation areas, gardens, and courts.[2] In such garden suburbs as Hamp-
stead and Earswick, and in the original Garden City

of Letchworth (all in collaboration with Barry
Parker), and in the British war housing communities,
Unwin worked out his concepts of low-density, large-
scale development later applied by Stein and Wright.
"We must work on the principle of grouping our
buildings and combining our open spaces," Unwin
explained, "having areas fairly closely built upon,
surrounded by others of open space, rather than that
of scattering and indefinitely mixing our buildings
and our spaces." [3]

Sunnyside did not represent the first significant application of Unwin's discovery that important economies and a superior residential environment were
inherent in the careful planning of large building
groups. Andrew J. Thomas, a New York architect,
was responsible for a major breakthrough in apartment house design in the 1920's. His path often
crossed that of the RPAA, and his thinking was
equally influenced by the postwar inflation of building costs which discouraged investment in low-
income housing.

Starting out as a realtor and general contractor,
Thomas evolved into an architect who viewed low-
and medium-priced rental housing as a technical
challenge and social necessity. Like Wright, Ackerman, and Kohn, Thomas had worked for the Emergency Fleet Corporation in the federal war housing
program. His greatest success came in 1922 when he
was selected to design the extraordinarily influential
Metropolitan Life Insurance apartments, but he had
been experimenting for several years with the so-
called "garden apartment" (not to be confused with
the row-type development which later usurped the

title). His earlier work was done for two progressive housing organizations, the limited-dividend City and Suburban Homes Company and the Queensboro Housing Corporation. Formed in 1896, the CSHC became the largest of all the semi-philanthropic corporations created to supply model tenements or houses. Extending back to at least the 1850's, the model housing tradition appealed to investors willing to serve the poor by accepting limited dividends and supplying superior accommodations. All the limited-dividend companies never accommodated more than a fraction of the poor, in New York or elsewhere, but they did pioneer in certain important structural and subdivision matters. Following the lead of Alfred T. White, whose three groups of Brooklyn model tenements between 1878 and 1890 greatly impressed contemporaries, the model tenement companies frequently broke away from the confines of the deep, narrow lot, grouping their units around a large central court and limiting apartments to two rooms in depth.

Completed by 1920, Thomas's work for the CSHC and Queensboro Corporation continued and improved upon this tradition of large-scale design and shallow-depth apartments. His Homewood buildings in Brooklyn for the CSHC covered approximately 50 per cent of the lot and contained a commodious interior "garden." In this case, however, Thomas did not use the block as his basic building unit. A superior lot coverage (only 38 per cent) was achieved by George H. Wells in a Queensboro Corporation apartment development in Queens, but the buildings occupied only one side of the street and lacked an interior court.[4] In another apartment group comprising ten units, also sponsored by the Queensboro Corporation, Thomas for the first time synthesized all the elements of the garden apartment: use of the block as the basic building unit; 50 per cent or less lot coverage; and the interior garden court.[5] Just as Unwin had achieved economies and a superior site plan by the elimination of streets and a more effective grouping of spaces, Thomas attained similar results through a reduction of non-rent paying space in the form of corridors, halls, and wasted room volume.

Thomas's reputation as the leading architect of moderate-rental garden-apartments soared upon completion of his Metropolitan Life Insurance project (1922–24), also in Queens. With the encouragement of the New York State Joint Legislative Committee on Housing, which urged insurance and other savings companies to take advantage of the tax exemption law and assist in alleviating the housing shortage, the Metropolitan decided to invest in an enormous development of some fifty apartment houses for 2,000 families.[6] The dwellings, five-story U-shaped walkups, covered 52 per cent of the land, and spread over several blocks. The open end of the U faced toward a central court stretching from street to street. Tax exemption made possible the low rentals of a maximum $9 per room per month.

Thomas had now demonstrated the superiority of a plan which used the block rather than the narrow lot as the building unit. Eliminating scattered, wasted space, which he grouped together in courts and gardens, Thomas produced an apartment which contained an equivalent amount of square feet of rentable space but covered a smaller percentage of the land. Following the success of his Metropolitan apartments, several other limited-dividend garden-apartments appeared, a development prominently identified with John D. Rockefeller, Jr. Choosing Thomas as his architect in all cases, Rockefeller launched his first venture in Bayonne, New Jersey. Thomas's apartments for the Bayonne Housing Corporation, begun in 1924, covered only 36 per cent of the land.[7] Rockefeller then commissioned Thomas to design an apartment on New York's East Side (Avenue A and 65th Street); it totaled 82 dwelling units and covered 56 per cent of the lot. Rentals of $12 to $15 a room exceeded those of the Metropolitan and Bayonne houses. Turning next to the Bronx, Rockefeller sponsored the Thomas Garden Apartments, named in honor of his architect. Located between Mott and Sheridan Avenues, on land purchased from the Ladies International Garment Worker's Union for a cooperative it had been unable to finance, the apartments covered less than 50 per cent of the lot and accommodated 175 families. Finally, Rockefeller chose Thomas to design his Paul Laurence Dunbar Apartments in New York's Harlem district. A rare acknowledgment of the special needs of New York's Negro population, the Dunbar development accommodated 511 families on the block bounded by 7th and 8th Avenues, 149th and 150th Streets. It covered 50 per cent of the land and contained a large garden court.

The garden apartment idea spread to Chicago in the late 1920's, where it influenced the design of the

Marshall Field and Michigan Boulevard Apartments. Located in the North Side, the Marshall Field development occupied two entire blocks; it contained 627 dwelling units renting at an average of $13 a room. Sponsored by the Julius Rosenwald Fund, the Michigan Boulevard Apartments were situated in the South Side. Covering an entire block and built for the benefit of Negroes, they contained 421 dwelling units and a garden court. Stein acted as consultant, in collaboration with Henry Wright.

The garden apartment idea of the 1920's, identified with Andrew J. Thomas, represented an effort to achieve economies and improvements in design and site-planning through use of the block as the basic building unit, reduced land coverage, compactness in design, grouping of open spaces into courts and gardens, and intensive cost analysis. In a limited way, Thomas provided a link between Unwin's ideas and the work of Stein and Wright at Sunnyside and Radburn. He had served as architectural consultant to Stein's Housing Committee of the Reconstruction Commission, and he had favorably impressed Frederick Ackerman even before the Metropolitan houses. Stein, who would employ Thomas's services at Radburn, considered his Metropolitan work a "great step forward." [8] Yet Thomas's influence upon the RPAA was diminished as a consequence of a crucial flaw—the persistence of the single lot as the subdivision unit. "Though Thomas came, in the end," according to Mumford, "to think of the block as the unit for apartment house development, his actual plans never entirely escaped from the invisible but potent constraint of the 20 x 100 foot city lot. . . . The members of Stein's group had a friendly relation with Thomas; but Wright and Stein, so far from being influenced by him, had from the start escaped his limitations; though they recognized his ability. . . ." [9] In other words, the RPAA saw in Thomas's U-shaped garden apartments only an improved variation of the small-scale, speculative building technique which they were attempting to discredit.

The RPAA received an opportunity to test its own theories at Sunnyside and Radburn, beginning in 1924 and 1928, respectively. Together with Thomas's garden apartments, these projects establish the 1920's as a period of major innovation in residential housing design. Sunnyside originated in 1923 when Stein convinced the New York realtor, Alexander M. Bing, to devote his immediate attention to housing rather than labor.[10] Accustomed to handling large real estate operations, Bing was an ideal sponsor for the City Housing Corporation, the limited-dividend company organized to carry out the proposal for a garden community which Bing, Wright, and Stein outlined in an unpublished report of 1923. In this report, they scrutinized in detail the social and economic advantages of a development which utilized large-scale, unified building techniques, and adapted Unwin's principles of residential design to the particular site.

With few exceptions, they found little in the American housing tradition to serve as precedents for their experiment. They complained, for example, that the predominant commercial channels had thoroughly failed to provide "adequate housing within the means of most workers," attributing the failure to the heavy carrying charges resulting from subdivision of vacant land far in advance of use, to the inefficiency of small-scale building operations, to restricted lot sizes necessitated by the limited capital of both builders and purchasers, and to extravagant street and block layouts.[11] A few recent commercial subdivisions, such as Guilford, Baltimore, and Shaker Heights, Cleveland, had incorporated the "decorative park" and avoided the monotonous and costly checkerboard, but these were too expensive for the clerical and manual workers the City Housing Corporation hoped to accommodate.

Bing, Wright, and Stein mostly found negative object lessons in the long tradition of American industrial new towns, with an occasional exception like Pullman, Illinois, providing a slight oasis in the dreary desert. The workers' homes were carefully designed, and the Company had supplied a variety of recreational and community facilities. More typical of industrial towns was Gary, Indiana, where the U. S. Steel Corporation, beginning in 1906, had established an industrial community in which housing and planning were subordinated to production. The Gary plan was conventional, "with uneconomically wide streets," and "too little land was set aside for residences and no provision was made for the protection of this area against undesirable development of the surrounding land." [12]

The early war contracts, labor mobility, and housing shortages in the period from 1914 to 1917 resulted in a number of developments which, in the opinion of Bing, Wright, and Stein, marked the first significant progress in industrial housing and provided precedents for the federal war housing. Pointing specifically to Neponset Garden Village of Bird and Sons of East Walpole, Massachusetts, Indian Hill Village of the Norton Grinding Company of Worcester, Massachusetts, Tyrone, New Mexico, sponsored by Phelps Dodge, and Kistler, Pennsylvania, where the Mount Union Refractories Company hired John Nolen as planner, they credited any improvement to the collaborative effort of planners, engineers, and architects, and to European influences upon "landscape and building design."

The period 1914–1917 also witnessed some progress in the character of industrial housing in or near existing towns. Bing, Wright, and Stein singled out the work of the Bridgeport Housing Company, organized in 1916, as the most satisfactory example. They were most impressed by the Company's efficient, centralized management, financing procedures, and experimentation with building types and groupings. It was in the federal war housing, however, that they discovered the most satisfactory American precedents for what they hoped to achieve themselves: "The houses in design and grouping, in many of the war towns, are far superior to past industrial housing in America, and compare favorably with the best European work. One advance over past methods was the bringing together in close co-operation of architect, town-planner and engineer in contrast with the usual method of calling in first engineer —then architect—and finally town-planner." [13] Such war developments as Yorkship Village in Camden,

New Jersey, and Buckman Village in Chester, Pennsylvania, stood in sharp contrast to the typical planning and housing arrangements of the industrial town where a "single badly designed unit was repeated indefinitely."

The City Housing Corporation was created to apply more systematically and efficiently the large-scale development principles first employed extensively in the federal housing of 1918–1919, and to demonstrate conclusively their economic and social superiority to past and present real estate operations. Both Sunnyside and Radburn have been described and illustrated innumerable times, nowhere better than in Stein's own *Toward New Towns for America,* and it is unnecessary to examine them in great detail here. We are concerned primarily with their general relationship to the broader community planning synthesis of the RPAA. Constructed between 1924 and 1928, Sunnyside was located on a 70-acre tract of land in Queens purchased from the Pennyslvania Railroad. Unable to persuade the Borough Engineer to modify the existing plat, Stein and Wright were forced to work within the confines of the gridiron street system, and thus the rectangular block. This was a serious handicap, considering the emphasis they had placed upon innovations in the street pattern in their unpublished proposal for a garden community. Indeed, such innovations were pivotal to their entire scheme, as their painstaking analysis of a model 640-acre tract demonstrated. Using the normal street plan, they calculated that the tract would contain 150 blocks, 200 x 600 feet in dimension. This would provide frontage for 7,000 25-foot lots, requiring 123,500 lineal feet of street (60 feet wide for the most part). Thus 193 acres or 32 per cent of the tract was consumed by streets. In comparison, the plan they proposed for the same tract provided for 70 blocks ranging from 600 to 1000 feet in length, requiring only 86,400 lineal feet of streets, differing in width and consuming only 135 acres, or 23⅓ per cent of the tract. They argued that their plan provided a superior residential environment, and saved $1,250,000 in the cost of improvements.[14]

Although forced to accept the rectangular block, Stein and Wright nonetheless eschewed the single-lot subdivision and used the one-, two-, and three-family row house as the leading motif at Sunnyside. The row groups ran along the perimeter of the block, or at right angles to the street, and enclosed a large central garden. Sunnyside also included a few apartment houses. The row dwellings ranged in price from about $8,000 for a single-family unit to $19,000 for the three-family. As a visit to Sunnyside today will confirm, the variation of roof types and heights, the interior gardens, the mixture of different kinds of housing, and the skillful grouping of building masses, all combined to create a development far superior to that of the average commercial builder.

The RPAA had expected that low-density, large-scale group housing, financed by low-interest capital, built rapidly to minimize carrying charges, and effecting economies through centralized purchase and management, would offer not only a superior residential environment, but a substantial reduction in costs as well. It bears repeating that the RPAA is significant both for its efforts to formulate the principles of good residential design and for its concern with reducing building costs at every possible point. Wright assumed the leadership in this matter. He analyzed in exhaustive detail the cost factors at Sunnyside, and it was he, Mumford explains, who "pointed out that a drop of one per cent in the rate of interest would effect a greater lowering of costs than all the cheeseparing that might be done on the structure; it was also he who demonstrated that every new technological development in the internal structure added costs which resulted in a further cramping of the space: or, as he put it, one room of the old-fashioned house is now buried in the street." [15] Since technological progress was inevitable, it was all the more necessary, in the eyes of the RPAA, to reduce costs by planning houses, streets, and utilities in a single, unified operation.

Yet despite Wright's laborious cost analyses and the actual economies effected through standardization, mass purchasing, and unified operations, Sunnyside houses in the end turned out to be more expensive than those of the speculative developer. For one thing, the refusal of the Borough Engineer to modify the gridiron system seriously thwarted potential economies in site-planning. For another, the six per cent dividend rate of the City Housing Corporation was moderate in comparison to the commercial market, but still not low enough to serve the needs of manual and clerical workers. Most important, Stein and Wright had not considered the overhead of large-scale operations in their calculations, an overhead which "often cancelled out the economies." They "knew better" by 1930, Mumford explains: "They still held it was important for unified design and for economies in site-planning, which are impossible when the individual lot, even when multiplied along a whole street front, is taken as the unit of design. But they had already discovered at Sunnyside that it was difficult, for all the supposed economies of buying wholesale, to compete with the ordinary speculative builder in pricing the individual house." The latter, who "carried his office in his hat," avoided the "costs of an expensive office in mid-town Manhattan, publicity experts, permanent sales staff, etc.—to say nothing of architects!" Mumford, who lived at Sunnyside for eleven years, concludes that the "Sunnyside buildings were better planned and were architecturally more comely, and had usable open space that the ordinary builder either swallowed up or wasted: but they weren't cheaper, and in some respects, they lacked conveniences that the speculator supplied." [16]

Sunnyside demonstrated the RPAA's proposition that large-scale design and site-planning could effect certain economies and produce a superior residential environment. In the case of Sunnyside, however, overhead expenses eliminated any possibility of accommodating low-income groups. Yet the RPAA's case for community planning did not rest exclusively upon its design hypotheses; it consisted of a series of interlocking propositions involving low-cost capital and regional planning, both of which offered potential economies which might compensate for increased overhead. Before considering these features of the RPAA's community planning program, it is necessary to look briefly at Radburn, the final achievement of the City Housing Corporation.

The Corporation acquired 1,258 acres in Fairlawn Borough, New Jersey, some seventeen miles from New York, for what was to be its Garden City. Beginning operations in 1928, it had erected 175 one-family homes, 10 two-family units and a garden apartment group for 92 families by the end of 1929. Radburn was not unique for any of its single features, as Stein points out, but for its synthesis of superblock, differentiated road system, separation of pedestrian and vehicular traffic, house turned inward, and interior park.[17] The superblocks of 30 to 50 acres and interior parks in the Corporation's "town for the motor age" were anticipated in less dramatic fashion in the English Garden City and suburb. The house turned inward represented a feature long favored by Wright, who had been experimenting for years with ways of arranging and relating houses in groups. The idea was modestly applied at Sunnyside, where some porches were located on the garden side of the house. As for Radburn's differentiated street system, Stein refers to precedents in the cul-de-sac of the English village and the American colonial village, while Olmsted and Vaux had pioneered in the separation of pedestrian and vehicular traffic in their plan for Central Park.[18]

Radburn by 1931 included 335 families, or a little over 1,000 inhabitants, and eventually accommodated some 400 families. It never approximated a genuine Garden City with industry, greenbelt, and cooperative land holding. Nonetheless Radburn, in which Stein, Wright, and their collaborators were liberated from the constrictions of the rectangular block, proved even more successful than Sunnyside as an object lesson in residential site-planning and design.[19] It represented a memorable response to the challenge posed to the community planner by the automobile and the increasing amount of leisure time available to the urban population. Radburn was planned deliberately to reconcile the automobile with residential amenity and safety, and to supply recreational facilities adequate to the changing ratio between work and leisure in modern life.[20] In this sense Radburn was significant as an experiment in applied sociology. Insulated from, but surrounded by the high-speed arterial road, it also suggested to Benton MacKaye the idea of the "townless highway," or the diversion of through traffic from cities and towns for the benefit of both motorist and community (thus avoiding the mistakes of the railroad engineers). Proposed in 1930, MacKaye's "townless highway" anticipated virtually every feature of the modern turnpike.[21]

One unfortunate consequence of the City Housing Corporation's failure to develop Radburn into a genuine Garden City or New Town was the lost opportunity for a broadly-conceived, controlled experiment in community planning, testing relationships between physical form and community organization. Before Radburn was begun, members of the RPAA devoted considerable time to analyzing the "physical equipment" of a "garden or regional city" including not only housing, but "industrial, governmental, educational, cultural, recreational, religious and social purposes." [22] The discussions at a conference at the Hudson Guild Farm in the fall of 1927 reveal that although members of the RPAA did not doubt the desirability of community or quanta planning, they possessed no dogmatic or unanimous views with regard to form, structure, or size. On size, for example, Stein offered no precise figures, remaining content with the observation that "increase beyond a certain point enormously complicated and heightened the costs of city life." Without necessarily committing himself to a 50,000 figure, Wright suggested that beyond that point a substantial investment in urban transportation would be required disproportionate to any community gains. The important consideration for Wright was that modern power and transportation technology reduced the need for self-sufficiency of any single urban unit and provided a basis for a regional grouping of cities and institutions.

Like size, community organization remained an open question, subject to the tests of experience and experiment. Members of the RPAA inclined to the belief that community planning would provide a sound physical basis for a more intense civic association, but they offered no definite schemes. Stein thought that Clarence Perry's community cell of 160 acres had some merit, but John Lovejoy Elliott protested that the "Community Man" had no more validity than the "Economic Man" of the classical economists, and that people would not be satisfied as members of any single community unit. Mumford, on the other hand, maintained that neighborhoods existed "whether people were conscious of them or not, and that failure to recognize their existence did not make people more free, but prevented them from doing effectively the things they were forced to do anyway." Related to the problem of community organization was the role of the development corporation, and here again uncertainty prevailed. Thus Herbert Emmerich, referring to experience at Sunnyside, initially advised caution in stimulating citizen organization and participation. The early formation of court units with boards of trustees to administer the open areas and ratify Company policy had, it seems, produced "friction and delay." But Emmerich admitted the advisability of some sacrifice of efficiency in favor of democratic expression after Elliott pointed out that the inhabitants needed training in community administration and that without some self-government they would become apathetic and suspicious of the Company.

Nothing was more essential to the success of the projected New Town than the establishment of an adequate economic base, but nothing was more elusive or complex than the procedures for stimulating industrial development. Contrasting Rochester with Buffalo, Stein pointed to the wage differential between skilled and heavy industry, adding that if large numbers of low-paid workers settled in the Garden City, then industry would have to subsidize their housing or raise their wages. Mumford warned that unless this issue was resolved somehow, a shantytown was sure to sprawl on the outskirts of the city. Complicating the entire issue was H. M. Propper's observation that trade unions would probably resist decentralization because of the obstacles it posed to labor organization.

The educational institutions of the future New Town engendered considerable controversy. Emmerich advised a conservative approach, eschewing a pioneering role and working with the existing system of public education. Mumford, however, thought that at least one modern, progressive school would attract desirable population groups to the community. His proposal aroused a general dissent with Emmerich objecting that Mumford's pacesetter would result in class divisions. As far as higher education was concerned, there was some support for a small college or technical school to help avoid what Wright described as the dangers of "dullness and provincialism." [23]

These many problems were not destined to be resolved at Radburn. They emerged as live issues again in connection with the community program of the Division of Subsistence Homesteads and Resettlement Administration in the 1930's, and the British New Towns program after World War II. If Radburn had developed as the Garden City anticipated by the City Housing Corporation and RPAA, perhaps these later community programs might have been spared numerous costly errors.

Chapter 5

Radburn not only failed to materialize as a New Town, but proved to be an economic disaster because of the depression, thus demonstrating no more than Sunnyside that large-scale development significantly reduced costs.[1] As we mentioned, however, the RPAA's approach to the problem of housing and development costs was never limited to innovations in site-planning scale and procedures alone; cost analysis pervaded its entire community planning synthesis resulting in a new conception of government's role in housing.

The City Housing Corporation, which limited dividends to 6 per cent, stood midway between the strictly commercial investor and the philanthropic fund and cooperative. Both the limited-dividend company and philanthropic fund had been devised around the mid-nineteenth century to supply better housing at lower rents for urban workers than the commercial developer could offer. Only a handful of philanthropic housing trusts, beginning with George Peabody's London "Donation Fund" in 1862, had been established. Other English examples included the Guinnes Trust and the Sutton Housing Trust, the Bournville Village Trust established by the cocoa manufacturer, George Cadbury, in 1900, and the Joseph Rowntree Trust of 1904 (for which Unwin and Parker designed Earswick Garden Suburb). Germany's garden suburb of Margarethenhöhe had been established under the auspices of the Margarethe Krupp Fund, and in the early twentieth century the Lebaudy and Rothschild Foundations were organized in Paris. In the United States the Mullanphy Apartments of St. Louis, sponsored by the Mullanphy Emigrant and Travelers Relief Fund, housed thirty-two families, and the Boston publisher, Edwin Ginn, sponsored the Charlesbank Homes in 1911 (a five-story building).[2] All of these funds, which existed prior to the formation of the City Housing Corporation, dispensed with stockholders and dividends entirely. The Fred L. Lavanburg Foundation, incorporated in 1927, built a large E-shaped apartment house on the lower East Side accommodating 110 families. Its project was particularly interesting as an experiment in enlightened management.[3]

Apart from an experimental and demonstration value (Cadbury's Bournville, for example, exerted a profound influence on American planners and housing reformers in the early twentieth century), the philanthropic trust was obviously useless as a financial or administrative device to supply low-cost housing in substantial quantities. The cooperative mechanism was more promising, but far more successful in Europe than in the United States, where labor support and government financial assistance were lacking. Many of the so-called "cooperatives" of the 1920's provided for joint management and ownership of common areas such as halls, but they did not preclude individual lease or sale of apartments at a profit. Private builders erected and sold them to individuals whose stock determined their voting power. In the genuine cooperative each member possessed one vote irrespective of capital holdings, and he owned stock in the organization rather than individual apartments; these belonged to the society, which possessed first option on redemption of stock.

The United States Bureau of Labor Statistics discovered only forty cooperative housing societies in existence during the mid-1920's. All but two of these were in New York City. The Bureau collected data on 32 of the societies—22 in Brooklyn, 9 in Manhattan, and 1 in Wisconsin. America's meager cooperative housing tradition, like the innovations in residential design described earlier, was distinctively a product of the 1920's. Only two of the societies were in operation before 1920. All of the New York cooperative dwellings were apartment houses, in contrast to the 105 individual homes erected by the Milwaukee Garden Homes Company. The New York cooperatives accommodated 2,073 families, mostly in Brooklyn and Manhattan; the Brooklyn societies were almost entirely composed of Finns and other Scandinavians.[4] Cooperative housing in the United States, representing one method of reducing costs or rentals, was not only scanty but frequently unsuccessful. The Milwaukee Garden Homes Company failed as a cooperative venture, and two apartments at Sunnyside sponsored by the Cooperative League proved less successful than dwellings for sale or rent.

Limited-dividend housing corporations accommodated far more families than philanthropic trusts and cooperatives taken together. "Investment philanthropy" in housing appeared in England as early as 1845 with the formation of the Metropolitan Association for Improving the Dwellings of the Industrial Classes and aroused some interest in the United States during the same decade. Lemuel Shattuck, for example, refers to a meeting of Boston citizens in 1846 resulting in a report recommending the "establishment of chartered or private companies, to procure the construction of large, well-fitted buildings, especially designed for the use of [the poorer class] of tenants." [5] The New York Association for Improving the Condition of the Poor, organized in 1843, was concerned with housing conditions from the start, and in the 1850's it sponsored a "Workmen's Home." Model tenement or housing companies appeared in Boston in the 1870's and the movement became firmly established with the success of Alfred T. White's "Home" and "Tower" Buildings in Brooklyn (1877–1879). Although the limited-dividend companies which appeared in the late nineteenth and early twentieth centuries often produced multi-family tenements, particularly in New York City, they were also responsible for one- and two-family homes in Boston, Cincinnati, Washington, D. C., and Philadelphia.

The families accommodated in the tenements and homes of the limited-dividend companies between the 1850's and the 1920's numbered in the thousands, but the commercial builder provided for the hundreds of thousands and millions. The City Housing Corporation differed from previous limited-dividend companies in that its sponsors sought to establish a permanent partnership between government and cooperative or limited-dividend organizations, wherein direct government financial assistance would increase the supply of low-cost capital available for non-commercial housing operations. In more general terms, the RPAA focused attention upon the relationship between the quantity and quality of housing, and the amount and cost of capital. Its members sharply challenged the traditional assumption that government's role in housing was limited to the enactment of minimum standards legislation. Throughout the 1920's the RPAA pressed for the establishment of financial mechanisms to channel government capital into the housing market to benefit income groups which existing lending and building institutions did not satisfactorily accommodate.

Clarence Stein assumed the pivotal role in the RPAA's efforts to increase the supply and diminish the cost of capital available for non-speculative housing. Since he is usually identified with Sunnyside and Radburn, few persons remember that Stein also served as the first and only chairman of the New York State Commission of Housing and Regional Planning (1923–26), a post he accepted on the explicit understanding that the Commission would deal with regional planning as well as housing.[6] Stein drew on the services of Mumford, who surveyed the various forms of government aid to housing in Europe, and Wright, who prepared a regional report on New York State in 1926, and MacKaye, who prepared studies of the economic flow from raw material to finished product.[7] The central challenge before the Commission, as Stein saw it, was this: "The standard that the public has required for its own protection has gradually risen. The ability of the individual to pay for that standard has diminished. Thus there has steadily grown up this divergence—this ominous parting of the ways—between the standard of house set by the community—the adequate house—and the inadequate incomes of those that cannot dwell in that house." [8]

At the time of the Reconstruction Commission (1919–20), Stein had not been aware of the precedents for constructive housing legislation established by the Massachusetts Homestead Commission, but he had been impressed by the proposals for government assistance included in the report of the Milwaukee Housing Commission.[9] The lines of influence, ultimately, trace mainly to Europe, which Stein visited in 1922 with Ernest Grunsfeld. He was particularly intrigued by Holland's response to the postwar housing crisis, as severe in Europe as in the United States. Holland's national housing legislation of 1901 had provided for loans to municipalities and housing societies of up to 100 per cent of development costs, and in 1919 additional legislation provided for subsidies to compensate for spiraling construction prices. Between 1918 and 1922 the City of Amsterdam was responsible for more than 3,000 houses completed or in process of construction, and the building societies for almost 7,000. Besides contributing part of the subsidy, Amsterdam assisted the public utility societies through lease of land which it had purchased. The quality of the housing developments greatly impressed Stein, who saw "not only unified blocks but whole sections of the city—groups of five or ten blocks . . . being created at one time" and all the housing types, whether one-, two-family or apartment, built "around great open courts." The contrast between Holland's government-aided community building and the rent controls and tax exemption measures of New York evoked sharp criticism from Stein. "This program [of the Reconstruction Commission]," he complained, "that would have seemed so feeble in Holland was altogether too revolutionary for New York. Rather no houses than take the business from the speculator. He must be revived and brought back into the building game"— even if it meant tax exemption for buildings where rooms rented for $20 or $30 a month.[10]

In a series of hearings and reports extending from 1923 to 1926, Stein's CHRP paved the way for New York State's intervention in the housing field. It is worth repeating once again that neither Stein nor the others in the RPAA ever viewed the housing problem exclusively in terms of a literal shortage of shelter. Their proposals for increasing the housing supply through tapping new sources of low-cost capital were always inseparable from their conception of large-scale residential design and site-planning. As far as they were concerned, a housing shortage had existed through most of the nineteenth century. The postwar crisis simply intensified a chronic shortage of good low-cost housing, and extended the shortage to middle-income groups. Permanent reform depended upon a measure of government credit and supervision aimed not only at increasing the housing supply, but its quality as well.

Complaining of a continued scarcity of private capital for housing purposes, Stein's CHRP recommended municipal loans, public housing, and a constitutional amendment authorizing state housing credits. These recommendations were made in spite of the widespread construction of one- and two-family homes for sale in New York City. The Commission charged that the monthly payments of $40 and up, in addition to carrying costs, placed these homes "beyond the means of the mass of the population." Equally important, the quality of the new housing fell below the Commission's standards. It observed that to "confine one's aims to merely cheaper houses leads to false economy and inadequate homes." Builders had indeed reduced immediate costs, but the "ultimate installation of public improvements and the high rate of deterioration of many of the miles of wooden houses built in Queens make it doubtful that any real economy has been effected. . . ." The fundamental problem, "that of providing adequate housing at low cost" for the 69 per cent of New York families with incomes below $2,500, was not being solved by "speculative enterprise." [11]

The CHRP, like the Reconstruction Commission, scrutinized the principal elements of capital and maintenance cost in housing. It drew attention to economies possible through tax exemption (but limited to non-speculative housing ventures), rationalization of the building industry (involving standardization of parts, quantity production of homes, and efficient management), and the rapid development of large tracts. However, any permanent, constructive program to increase the supply and quality of housing depended, in the end, upon satisfactory financing procedures.

The major sources of mortgage funds at the time included savings banks, life insurance companies, savings and loan associations, trust companies, and private individuals and estates. The Commission found that the financing problem hinged not upon the six per cent first mortgages supplied through these agencies, but upon the financing of the balance not covered by the first mortgage. Including the interest on all mortgages, average money costs for commercial housing enterprises totaled 9 per cent, or "at least 8 per cent and in some cases . . . as high as 10 or 11 per cent." [12] Looking back to the 1920's, Mumford places considerable stress upon the relationship between the commercial lending situation and the postwar housing crisis: "The housing shortage was a real one; and there is no doubt that this helped in bringing public support to the movement [for government aid]. The shortage was unnecessarily prolonged, I think, because of an over-cautious lending policy on the part of the banks and loan societies; but then there were no mortgage guarantees at that time; and the largest gains from loans were made on second and third mortgages. Even the fact that the Metropolitan Life had begun investing in model apartment houses did not loosen the purse-strings sufficiently till after 1925; a much longer lapse than should have happened after the war. . . ." [13] Arguing that commercial lending agencies were simply unequipped to supply the capital at low interest rates necessary to accommodate the majority of families whose incomes totaled $2,500 or less, the CHRP pressed for a solution through "non-speculative enterprise which takes a moderate return on its investment." [14]

Referring to the successful, but limited achievements of the City and Suburban Homes Company, the City Housing Corporation, and the Metropolitan Life Insurance Company, the CHRP complained that these and similar organizations were seriously handicapped by a shortage of money for housing purposes. If supplied with adequate low-interest capital, they could "care for the needs of a large part of the underlying population whose income is less than $2,500." [15] To satisfy the capital needs of the limited-dividend companies destined, presumably, to supply the majority of the population with good housing, the CHRP proposed an ambitious program of government credits. It recommended the creation of a State Housing Board with supervisory powers, and a State Housing Bank which would finance the limited-dividend companies in such a way as to reduce the "excessive cost of securing capital, the principle contributing factor in the present cost of housing." For any given project, the company would have to contribute an equity equal to one-third of the total cost. The remainder would be raised through sale of state housing bonds at a rate not exceeding 5 per cent. Analogous to farm loan bonds, the housing bonds would be exempt from federal and state taxation, and secured by a first lien on the property. The act establishing a state housing bank would limit corporation dividends to 6 per cent and authorize municipalities to except their projects from taxation.

Much to the Commission's disappointment, the New York State Housing Law of 1926 eliminated the housing bank.[16] It established a State Housing Board, exempted the limited-dividend projects approved by the Board from state taxes and fees, restricted dividends to 6 per cent, and authorized municipalities to exempt projects from local taxation. Maximum rents were set at $12.50 per room per month in Manhattan, $11 in Brooklyn and the Bronx, $10 in the other boroughs and first class cities of the state, and $9 elsewhere. Although less than Stein and the CHRP desired, the Housing Law of 1926 was superior to the tax exemption measure of 1920, a speculator's bonanza which stimulated housing construction but did not benefit lower-income groups. However, a housing law which carried no provision for a housing bank to supply low-interest capital eliminated any possibility whatever that a significant portion of accommodations for low- and middle-income groups would be supplied by non-speculative agencies. The Law of 1926 represented an acknowledgment of, but half-hearted response to the fact that commercial builders and lending agencies were not reaching the majority of families whose incomes totaled $2,500 a year or less.

Yet it is doubtful that a state housing bank would

have radically affected the situation. Neither the CHRP nor anyone else offered evidence that large numbers of potential investors stood poised, ready to accept safe, but limited dividends in lieu of the less assured, but much higher profits available in commercial building.[17] A state housing bank might have resulted in more limited-dividend and cooperative housing than was the case, but there was no justification for assuming that significant structural changes would have occurred in the building industry. The concept of housing as a commodity subject to the laws of supply and demand, and provided by commercial entrepreneurs, was strongly ingrained in this country. Most of the direct and indirect government aids or subsidies since the 1930's have been designed to bolster the private building industry rather than transfer initiative to noncommercial cooperative or limited-dividend companies.

Although the government aid-to-housing programs since the 1930's (including public housing) differ in purpose and results from what the RPAA intended, they confirm its allegation that government financial intervention in housing had become an economic and social necessity. Even if it was unrealistic to hope, given the institutional and ideological blocks, that a substantial portion of low- and middle-income housing could be supplied on a nonspeculative basis, there was nothing unrealistic in the RPAA's contention that government economic assistance had become unavoidable.[18]

The New York State Board of Housing, established to administer America's first limited-dividend law, engaged in intensive research on housing design and costs to demonstrate the superiority of large-scale development and justified its work in terms of the chronic shortage of good, new housing whose rooms rented for under $15 a month.[19] The Board recommended Thomas's Metropolitan apartments as a model for the kind of housing which sponsors should erect under the auspices of the housing law. Among the advantages which it claimed for these apartments—"the outstanding example since the war of apartment construction for rents as low as $9 per room per month"—were "large scale operation, uniform standards of construction and improved facilities represented by the planning and mechanical equipment of the apartments and the relative openness of rear courts with space for landscaping and gardening." [20]

New York, it turned out, became the only city to take advantage of the State Housing Law. It enacted a measure in 1927 which exempted from taxation for twenty years the buildings and improvements of limited-dividend companies whose projects were approved by the State Board of Housing. The Amalgamated Housing Corporation, sponsored by the Amalgamated Clothing Workers of America, was first in the field. It constructed a group of six apartment houses in the Bronx (six-story walk-ups), which accommodated 303 families and surrounded an interior garden court. In 1928 the State Board of Housing approved three additional projects. The Farband Housing Corporation, sponsored by the Jewish National Workers Alliance of America, erected an apartment development in the Bronx containing 128 dwelling units. Both the Amalgamated and Farband houses were cooperatives. In Brooklyn the Chamber of Commerce appointed a citizens' committee (whose chairman, Louis Pink, was a member of the State Board of Housing), which sponsored the Brooklyn Garden Apartments. A single building, designed by the ubiquitous Thomas, accommodated 164 families. Finally, the Amalgamated, pleased with its initial experiment, acquired an adjacent site in order to construct another building containing 203 dwelling units and surrounding a central court 103 x 96 feet in dimension.

The Amalgamated launched a third project in 1930. It acquired at cost a tract in the lower East Side which had been purchased by Lieutenant-Governor Lehman and Aaron Rabinowitz, a member of the State Board of Housing. The Amalgamated Dwellings, Inc. then erected a building containing 234 apartments and the usual inner court. In order to assist families in acquiring apartments on the cooperative plan, Lehman and Rabinowitz offered to loan the necessary capital. The Brooklyn Garden Apartments Company sponsored a second project in 1930. Located in the Navy Yard district, it was a five-story walk-up containing 111 dwelling units. Since 1926 only three cooperative or limited-dividend companies, responsible for six separate developments, had taken advantage of the State Housing Law.[21]

In retrospect, the activities of the New York State Board of Housing are significant mainly as an effort to combine government financial aid (tax exemption) with high supervisory standards (adherence of sponsors to large-scale operation and good site-planning) and research into housing costs and design. Thus the Board followed in the tradition of the Massachusetts Homestead Commission and applied in practice two of the three key elements in the RPAA's community planning program. The Board's explicit policy was to "discourage applications for developments which do not offer a marked advance over available housing and which might in a short period of time be regarded as sub-standard." It insisted, therefore, upon a lot "sufficiently large to afford unobstructed light and air on all sides of the building," claiming that the large development was "not only better, but . . . cheaper." Equally important, the Board required that "building coverage be low enough to enable the reservation of adequate spaces between buildings for gardens and playgrounds." [22] It is unfortunate that later government housing agencies have often opposed rather than encouraged experimentation, and have not emulated the enlightened policy of the New York State Board of Housing in which government aid was combined with leadership in research and the formulation of high standards of design and site-planning. [23]

The cooperative apartments of the Amalgamated and Farband Companies proved to the satisfaction of the Board of Housing that with state aid "families to whom home ownership is otherwise beyond hope of realization, can actually become home owners." The extension of the cooperative principle from the economic to the social sphere in these same developments also attracted the Board's attention. An educational committee under a trained director at the Amalgamated endeavored to "give expression of the common interests derived from joint social ownership and a common social background and ideals." [24] The cooperative organization at the Amalgamated houses sponsored a kindergarten, a library, a gymnasium, and tea rooms. In addition, two cooperative stores served the tenants. At the Farband apartments similar provision was made for an auditorium, a gymnasium, a school, a library, and a cooperative store, all of which it was hoped would aid in welding the tenants into a cohesive social unit. This consideration for the domestic, cultural, and recreational needs of tenants represented a partial, limited expression of the social goals central to the community planning program of the RPAA. In nurturing the growth of the regional city, the Association hoped to universalize what MacKaye described as the "community of definite social structure, developing within certain geographic confines around a common civic purpose." [25]

The RPAA considered city planning inseparable from regional planning and viewed both in relation to definite community objectives. Maintaining that the physical and social character of cities were profoundly influenced by the wider regional distribution of population, resources, and institutions, the RPAA was exceptional for its willingness to pose fundamental questions about the planning function in modern society and the structure and purpose of cities.

Chapter 6

THE ORIGINS OF regionalism were complex, involving a European tradition transmitted by Mumford and an American tradition personified in MacKaye. An avowed disciple of the Scottish biosociologist and planner Patrick Geddes, whom he personally introduced to members of the RPAA in 1923, Mumford's regionalism was shaped also by Geddes' colleague, Victor Branford, the geographer George Perkins Marsh, and the "French regionalists, like Charles Brun and the whole school of French regional geographers."[1] In MacKaye's case, the lines of influence, direct and indirect, traced from the New England colonial village and Thoreauean naturalism through the regional ecology of John Wesley Powell, Nathaniel Shaler, and William Morris Davis, and into the conservationist technicism of Gifford Pinchot. Together Mumford and MacKaye formulated a regionalism which was partly romantic-poetic myth and aspiration, partly cultural revolt, and partly realistic response to the possibilities and challenges of a new technology epitomized in the automobile and electric power.

The French regionalism which Mumford conveyed to the RPAA was the strongest and most-self-conscious movement of its kind in Europe, the inheritor of the Rousseauian and literary Romanticism of an earlier period. In the 1850's a group of poets in Provence calling themselves *félibres* united in an effort to revive Provençal customs and language. Frédéric Mistral assumed leadership of the *félibristes,* who dedicated themselves to the resurrection of medieval provincial culture. A protest against the administrative and cultural centralization of France since the Revolution, regionalism spread in the 1860's when the earlier objections of Tocqueville and Comte were reinforced by such diverse figures as Le Play, Proudon, Duc de Broglie, and Prévost-Paradol. A cultural regionalism, similar to that of Provence, was launched in France-Comté by Charles Beauquier, who founded the weekly *Doubs* in 1869 and later published a dictionary of the regional language and a collection of folk songs. Before the end of the century Charles Le Goffic founded a Union Régionaliste Bretonne and Maurice Barrès, who championed a regional system of education from elementary school to university, promoted the movement in Lorraine. The geographer Vidal de la Blanche played an important role in directing academic attention to the significance of regions in French life.

In 1900 regionalists and decentralists formed the Féderation Régionaliste Française, which went beyond a sentimental romanticism and antiquarianism in an effort to establish the region as the basis for French administrative, judicial, economic, intellectual, and cultural life. *Le Régionalisme* by Charles Brun, a leader in the F.R.F., constituted a landmark in the theory and philosophy of regionalism. The Ligue de Répresentation Professionelle et d'Action Régionaliste, formed in 1913, lent its support to the movement under the leadership of Jean Hennessy.[2]

If French regionalism directed Mumford's attention to the possibilities of cultural and administrative decentralization, Patrick Geddes supplied him with a biological and sociological rationale. It was Geddes who originally distinguished between the paleotechnic and neotechnic machine ages (to which Mumford later added the eotechnic to precede the paleotechnic and the biotechnic to succeed the neotechnic). The paleotechnic nineteenth century—"Kakotopia"—Geddes criticized as an age which measured progress in terms of infinite quantitative expansion. According to him it lacked social or biological norms by which to direct and control its technology: "As paleotects we make it our prime endeavour to dig up coals, to run machinery, to produce cheap cotton, to clothe cheap people, to get up more coals, to run more machinery, and so on; and all this essentially towards 'extending markets.' "[3] Geddes condemned the paleotechnic as an exploitive era, wasteful of both human and natural resources, whose symbols were the coal pit, slag heap, and, above all, the slum. Indeed, the slum was the distinctive social contribution of the paleotechnic economy, based on coal and steel and directed toward the "private dissipation of resources." It produced a superslum for the urban and rural poor, and a semi-slum for more prosperous workers whose wives drudged out "all their days" in "long dormitory rows" with their "mean, wee backyards."

In contrast to the paleotechnic, the nascent neotechnic order was distinguished by a reorientation in goals from the "money gains of man to the vital budget of woman." Symbolized by the electric generator rather than the coal mine and steam engine, the neotechnic order substituted the unity of "place, work, and folk—environment, function, and organism"—for the one-dimensional material quantification of the paleotechnic.[4]

Geddes coined the phrase "conurbation" to describe the sprawling complex of paleotechnic urbanism: mill, factory, gutted coal mine, slum, dormitory suburb. For this he wished to substitute an urban structure with form and intense civic association which, "starting from its fundamentals, of port and road, of market and depot; and from its essentials, too, of family dwellings worthy to be permanent and hereditary homes . . . develops onwards to the supreme organs of the city's life—its acropolis and forum, its cloister and cathedral."[5] For Geddes the city, at its best, was a theater, an artifact in which a "civic drama" was staged allowing each individual to express his life with "fullness and adequacy." The only town planning equal to the challenge of the neotechnic city would be a "veritable orchestration" in which physical design blended with the social sciences and biological and social arts.

The unification of environment, function, and organism to which Geddes aspired required a regional framework of planning. The older borough and county councils, he contended, could no longer cope with such regional and inter-regional tasks as water supply and sanitation; nor could the neo-technic urban order, "characterised by electricity, hygiene, and art, by efficient and beautiful town planning," be disassociated from corresponding rural development. It was only through a unified view of town and country that one could plan for distinctively neotechnic equilibrium, balance, limits, and norms. The biological and organic analogies so conspicuous in the thinking of Mumford and the RPAA derived in good measure from Geddes' curious bio-sociology, which likened the city to an organism with its own laws of growth and development.[6]

As one who viewed the structure and function of cities from a regional perspective, Mumford always emphasized regional relationship and process far more than ideal plans or forms. Indeed, he complained that the Garden City as conceived and applied in England had fallen into a rut; it had become an "isolated *objet d'art*" and would remain so until the emphasis shifted from the concrete objective of a garden city to larger aims: industrial decentralization, relocation of population in "regional centers," and, most important, an entirely new orientation "radically different from that which produces as its typical product the urban-congestion-pyramid of which many of us are so proud."[7]

The most comprehensive statement of the regional ideal expounded by Mumford in the 1920's appeared in his three essays for the *Sociological Re-*

view, an English journal edited by Victor Branford. Focusing upon the region as a geographic fact transcending in importance any arbitrary political boundaries, Mumford defined the natural region as a variable located between the continental land mass and the historic village. Geology, land contour, and climate combined to create for each region, as delineated by ecologists and regional geographers, a unique configuration. The natural region fostered a certain type of vegetation and animal life and a discernible communal pattern, as in the case of the small, dispersed communities grouped around the waterfall of an upland. If the ecology of a region, its balance of population and resources was upset, this was often the consequence of human institutions, "like the operation of the financial credit system or exploitation for profit." Mumford, however, never assumed naively that human institutions as such represented an alien intrusion in some idyllic natural equilibrium. His quarrel was with those institutions and practices which misused or wasted either the human or natural resource potential of a region.

Like Geddes', the weight of Mumford's criticism fell upon the paleotechnic nineteenth century. Not only, he complained, did the extractive processes of the era waste and appropriate for private use the common resources of the earth, but they poisoned it as well by their "destruction of the beauty of the landscape," pollution of streams and drinking water, and filling of the air with a "finely divided carboniferous deposit," affecting life and vegetation for the worse. Rapid concentration of industrial production

along railroad and port termini accelerated the disintegration of the regional economy and ecology as
the "city grew at the expense—economical and
moral—of the countryside." Metropolitan centralization was stimulated by financial and credit institutions as well as the tendency for industry to cluster
round its sources of fuel, labor, and markets.
Centralization facilitated administrative control, and
financiers benefited from congestion and apprecia-
tion of land values.

Much as the coal, steam power, railroad complex
of the nineteenth century had encouraged centralization of production in large factory units in the
vicinity of metropolitan areas, twentieth-century
technology provided, in Mumford's view, a sound
basis for decentralization and regional reconstruction. This would depend in good measure upon the
deliberate use of electric power and the automobile
as instruments of regionalism. The decentralization
to which Mumford aspired, it is important to note,
implied neither the removal of single factories to
suburbs or open country, nor the shifting of a group
of factories or an industry from one place to benefit from cheap labor elsewhere, nor a reduction in the
size of large cities alone, nor least of all, a low-
density suburban diffusion. On the contrary, a comprehensive regionalism implied centralization as
much as its opposite. Use of the region as a planning
unit involved a unified program leading to the
"building up of old centres, the breaking-up of congested centres, and the founding of entirely new centres to promote social life, industry, culture. . . ."

Regionalism, or the regional city, suggested process more than form. Mumford hoped that it would result in a symbiotic rather than a parasitic relationship between city and country, and a satisfactory regional distribution of population, resources, and institutions. He set forth no abstract criteria for the urban concentrations forming the regional nodes: "No one size of city, and no one type of city, is sufficient to any region; the amount of concentration needed differs according to the place-possibility and the type of work; it ranges from the hamlet or village to serve the farming community to the regional capital, which acts as the centre for regional administration, for business, and for the higher branches of education—as well as for the specialized function not necessary for the smaller centre, such as the hospital and the higher courts of law."

Underlying Mumford's entire regional construct was the assumption that minima and maxima population groupings existed, not in any abstract or arbitrary sense but rather as a function of regional agricultural and commercial-industrial development on the one hand, and of a rich and diverse community life on the other. The modern metropolis and suburb, in his estimation, served neither the long-range economic nor the social needs of the regional population. Suburban diffusion desecrated the landscape and produced partial communities, lacking form or a sound economic and cultural base. In the case of the metropolis, an excessive amount of capital poured into expensive transportation systems and other utilities, thus increasing congestion by raising the value and forcing a more intensive use of the land; congestion and high real estate values, in turn, discouraged liberal reservation of land for public and community purposes and made it increasingly difficult to house the population adequately. Thus neither metropolitan centralization nor low-density suburban fragments and satellites could substitute, in Mumford's eyes, for community-building within the regional framework.[8]

Supplementing the European regional philosophies and traditions introduced by Mumford was the authentically American naturalist and conservationist heritage embodied in Benton MacKaye, who was born in New York City in 1879 but raised in Shirley Center, Massachusetts. While at Harvard, MacKaye had come under the influence of the geographers, Nathaniel S. Shaler and William M. Davis. Following his graduation in 1901 he became a forester, receiving an M.A. in 1905.[9] Like Thoreau, MacKaye possessed a deep affinity for nature; it was a romance which had begun with his childhood strolls through New England woods and fields. He described Thoreau as the "philosopher of environment," who penetrated the "eternities of the indigenous" and foresaw the "inroadings of the metropolitan." Through such figures as Powell and Marsh (indirectly), Shaler and Pinchot (at firsthand), MacKaye inherited a conservationist ecology aimed at the restoration and maintenance of balance among man, land, and resources (analogous to Geddes' unity of environment, function, and organism).

In 1864—fourteen years before Major Powell issued his classic report on the arid regions of the West advising revolutionary changes in land classification, use, and tenure—Marsh published his monumental *Earth as Modified by Human Action.* This was a loud protest against man's wanton misuse of land and resources and his failure to compensate for the disruption of nature's equilibrium. A pioneer, expansionist society, however, was not disposed to believe that the earth was given to man "for usufruct alone, rather than consumption," and still less for "profligate waste." Man everywhere, not simply in the United States, was a disturbing agent, Marsh complained; wherever he settled he destroyed the organic balance and did so in direct ratio to his level of civilization. It seemed that nature's revenge offered the only hope for conservation and restoration. One day man would learn that in destroying the forest he eliminated the natural reservoir of moisture stored in its vegetable mould and reaped a legacy of parched dust. To what degree, Marsh wondered, can man "permanently modify and ameliorate those physical conditions of terrestrial surface and climate on which his material welfare depends; how far [can he] compensate, arrest, or retard the deterioration which many of his agricultural and industrial processes tend to produce; how far [can he] restore fertility and salubrity to soils which his follies or his crimes have made barren or pestilential?" [10] Echoing Marsh half a century later, Shaler thundered out against the desecration of the landscape: "With the first step upward . . . and ever in increasing measure as he mounts toward civilization, man becomes a spoiler." His agriculture subverted the "ancient order of the soils," uprooting the protective plant mantle and exposing the earth to destructive erosion. [11] In cases of unusually destructive tillage, deportation of soil occurred far more rapidly than its restoration through rock decay, and soluble minerals were consumed at an excessive rate.

MacKaye supported Pinchot in his effort to bring America's natural resources under the control of experts and technicians who would substitute a policy of conservation and scientific, efficient utilization for the waste and thoughtless exploitation of the pioneer past. Thoreauean naturalism, conservationist ecology and technicism, the eotechnic balance of man, land, and resources epitomized in the New England colonial village—all entered into Mac-Kaye's regionalism. A good deal of conservationist history has been written in which little or no mention is made of MacKaye, an unfortunate oversight considering that this gaunt New Englander, employed in the Forest Service of the U. S. Department of Agriculture, possessed a prophetic and fertile imagination rarely equalled in the conservationist tradition. An indefatigable community-builder, MacKaye was a striking combination of romantic and geo-technician.

In the outline and summary he prepared of the U. S. Department of Labor's policy on "employment and natural resources," MacKaye applied his imagination to a scheme which surely ranks among the most mature and memorable fruits of the American conservation movement. Published in 1919, but prepared in part while he was a member of the Forest Service, MacKaye's report climaxed a "general investigation of land as an opportunity for workers" begun in 1915 by the Labor Department. MacKaye envisioned nothing short of a national program of community-building whose corollary benefits included preservation and efficient utilization of the national domain, full employment, and the complete reorganization of the farming, lumbering, and mining industries.

Encompassing agricultural land, forests, mineral and water resources, MacKaye's scheme was distinctive for its unification of communitarianism with conservationist ecology and technicism. In the case of agriculture, MacKaye proposed the substitution of colonization or community settlement based upon careful prior survey and classification for the traditional individualistic type. This policy, combined with tenure dependent upon use, he contrasted to the homestead principle that "raw land without improvements is all the settler needs wherewith to make for himself a farm and a home." Australia provided MacKaye with a colonization model:

Agriculture under this system is handled through the community unit as against the isolated farm unit. Not only is each farm prepared for use through initial cultivation of the soil and the erection of farm buildings but the community itself is organized for cooperative action in marketing produce, purchasing supplies, obtaining credit, and in providing for social as well as economic needs. Hence a portion of land is usually reserved at the center of each community for the location of cooperative warehouses, stores, and banks, as well as for schools and churches. At or near this center a demonstration farm may be established on which purebred cattle and other stock are raised and sold at cost to settlers; and this farm may also be used as a training school for incoming settlers.[12]

As North American precedents for a colonization system, MacKaye cited the returned-soldier colony at

Kapuskasing in northern Ontario and the Durham colony of the California Land Settlement Board.

Community and conservation were likewise central to MacKaye's proposals for forest and mineral resources. To establish lumbering on a sound economic and family basis, in lieu of the "timber mining" and migratory labor of the past, MacKaye emphasized the need for long-range planning and timber-culture comparable to that of the state-owned forests in Europe. Each timber area would have to supply a continuous, pre-determined annual yield, thus making feasible the establishment of permanent, nearby communities (not migratory camps) for the men and their families. As for coal and other minerals, MacKaye argued that the "mining community, organized perhaps in connection with an agricultural unit, could replace the typical 'mining camp.' "

Reorganization of agriculture, lumbering, and mining, and efficient development of water resources for "sanitation, irrigation, navigation, power," hinged ultimately upon a jealous safeguarding of the public domain. The permanent reservation of government agricultural, forest, and mineral land as well as water rights would provide extensive opportunities for communitarian and resource development and serve, hopefully, as a model for private interests. To carry out the plans a national board was needed to cooperate with states, reserve water rights and the public domain, survey and classify lands for most efficient use, acquire private land through condemnation proceedings or otherwise, build and supervise the various colonies, and organize cooperative facilities within them. The board would have at its disposal a "construction service" to supply necessary labor.

Nothing approximating MacKaye's plan for systematic community-building, conservation, and resource development ever materialized, although it foreshadowed a substantial corpus of New Deal legislation. He soon prepared a more modest but nonetheless bold proposal for an Appalachian Trail which he presented to Stein when Whitaker introduced them at the Hudson Guild Farm in the summer of 1921. An idea which evolved from his scouting and walking expeditions in the company of Sturgis Pray many years before, MacKaye's scheme entailed a series of recreational communities in the Appalachians, connected by a walking trail and stretching from New England to Georgia, or from Mt. Washington to Mt. Mitchell. It included shelter camps comparable to those already established in the White and Green Mountains, cooperative community camps, and food and farm camps in adjoining valleys or combined with the community camps. Planned to fit into broader programs of regional planning and architecture, the community camps constituted the nucleus of the entire proposal. MacKaye hoped they would offer a Thoreau-like "sanctuary and . . . refuge from the scramble of every-day worldly commercial life," providing opportunities for a wide range of non-industrial pursuits: contemplation, study, recreation, and education.[13] The Committee on Community Planning of the American Institute of Architects adopted and fostered the Appalachian Trail.[14] Following the formation of the RPAA in 1923, which also endorsed the project, an effort was made to link the Trail with the revival of country dances and mountain ballads.[15]

Later in the decade MacKaye directed his attention to a different kind of regional scheme. He assisted the Russian Reconstruction Farms in the preparation of a report on the Archangelskoe Rayon Region in order to demonstrate the probable effect of American agricultural techniques upon local production, labor needs, and land use. Stein and Wright contributed to this study by sketching the typical "artel" or "small community working unit" adopted by MacKaye as the basis for community development.[16]

Only in part a romantic attitude compounded of naturalism and a yearning for provincial cultural expression, the regionalism of the RPAA also involved a sharp critique of metropolitan centralization comparable to that of the French regionalists and a philosophy of organic, administered community-building inspired by Geddes' bio-sociology and Howard's Garden City. One curious contribution of the English Garden Cities of Letchworth and Welwyn to American regionalism was the publication of the Regional Plan Number of *The Survey Graphic* (*Survey*) in 1925. It was almost rejected by editor Paul Kellogg because it presumably dealt with abstractions and ideas rather than concrete facts. The existence of the English Garden Cities, however, helped in persuading Kellogg to publish the issue.[17]

Edited by Mumford, the Regional Plan Number

was prepared "by people who were loth to live fractional lives in either city or country—and refuse to admit that civilization requires of them perpetually the sacrifices they must make today to reconcile the means to live with a way of living." A common criticism of the industrial-commercial metropolis and a common preference for a regional planning which conceived of "people, industry and the land as a single unit," linked the diverse articles. Adopting New York as the archetype of the "dinosaur city," Stein tried to explain why metropolitan life had become incompatible with a humane existence. The answer lay in the colossal "overheads" entailed in the mere physical survival of the large city. The creation and maintenance of elaborate transportation, water, waste-disposal, and other utility systems, and the effects of congestion and inflated land values upon housing diverted "money and effort which should go into making the city more livable —the money that should be spent on the education of children, on the maintenance of health, upon art, education, and culture—all this money and effort is devoted to expenditures which do no more than make the physical side of congestion barely tolerable." [18]

Employing the same "overhead" critique, Stuart Chase explained what seemed to him the advantages of a regionally organized system of production and distribution. Pointing to the lack of correlation between factory location and sources of raw materials, he advised a more efficient and less wasteful regrouping of population into communities or regions "specifically planned for the maximum of local sub-

sistence and the minimum of cross-hauling. . . ."
One of Mumford's articles described the superior
system of social organization which paralleled the
alleged economic benefits of regionalism. "Our present congested districts," he insisted, "are the results
of the crude applications of the mechanical and
mathematical sciences to social development; our
garden cities represent the fuller development of the
more human arts and sciences—biology and medi-
cine and psychiatry and education and architecture."
Planning for communities limited in size and population represented the application of technics to the
culture of life in contrast to metropolitanism with its
paleotechnic oblivion to norms. The influence of
Geddes' bio-sociology is apparent in Mumford's
contrast between metropolitan and regional planning. He condemned metropolitanism as an inorganic, crystal-like growth by accretion—"the mechanical addition of blocks and avenues to the
original center, proceeding automatically and without limit." Regionalism, by contrast, suggested an
organic, cell-like fission resulting in new population
centers with their own nuclei of civic institutions and
"norm of development." [19]

The RPAA already recognized in the 1920's that
a substantial dispersion of population and industry
to suburban areas would be accelerated by electric
power and the gasoline engine. It viewed the issue
as one of controlled, regional decentralization—an
administered function of modern society—or of
formless dispersion in which the suburbs would
sooner or later be "swallowed up and lost in the
maw of the great city." [20] Indeed, its entire regional

scheme hinged upon the social policies devised to control the effects of electric power and the auto.

The electrical industry in the United States had been launched in 1882 when a generating plant transmitted current to a few hundred sixteen-candle-power bulbs distributed among less than a dozen buildings on New York's Pearl Street. One of the earliest experiments in long-distance power transmission occurred the following decade, when an eighteen-mile line operating under an 11,000 volt pressure opened in California. As early as 1902, the output of central power stations in the United States had reached 2,506,800,000 kilowatt hours, a figure which rose to 38,288,300,000 two decades later.[21] The RPAA emphasized that electric power opened revolutionary possibilities for industrial location since it liberated the factory from both the coal mine and waterfall. The electric generator could transmit power over long distances far more efficiently than the steam engine, which operated nearby machinery by means of connecting belts or shafts.

The extensive use of electrical power by the 1920's raised serious problems of government and social policy. Members of the RPAA became intimately identified with the crusade for "giant power," or the creation of an electric power grid conducive to the rejuvenation of country life and the reversal of metropolitan centralization. Giant power aroused considerable interest in Pennsylvania, where Governor Pinchot appointed the engineer, Morris Llewellyn Cooke, to direct a Giant Power Survey Board. As summarized by Cooke, giant power objectives included the establishment of large steam-generating stations located at or near mines and supplying current to trunk transmission lines with a 220,000 volt capacity, the integration and coordination of facilities for the supply, transmission, and distribution of electric power, the full development of water power resources, the recovery of coal by-products, rural and railroad electrification, rate reduction to small consumers, and public direction of the entire system in the public interest. Public supervision was indispensable, Pinchot maintained, as electric power represented a "gigantic monopoly" over the "greatest industrial fact of our time." If rightly used, electric power would contribute to a social revolution based upon a redistribution of population and industry: "Steam brought about the centralization of industry, a decline in country life, the decay of many small communities, and the weakening of family ties. Giant Power may bring about the decentralization of industry, the restoration of country life, and the upbuilding of the small communities and of the family." [22]

The Canadian province of Ontario provided Pinchot, Cooke, MacKaye, Robert Bruère, and other giant power leaders with a model for enlightened public policy. Almost 400 municipalities in Ontario had cooperatively invested in a giant power system which supplied electricity at low rates. [23] "Decentralization and the increasing attractiveness of the small town and farm," according to Bruère, "have been conspicuous results of large scale electrical development in the Province of Ontario." [24] In the Regional Plan Number of the *Survey,* Bruère elaborated upon the implications of giant power for region-building. It was the key to the integration of farm, town, and city, the instrument through which the "social engineer" might correct the "present abnormalities and diffuse the advantages of each." Regional planning, linked with the giant power grid, offered correctives to both the "lop-sided industrial life of our slum-breeding cities and the hard, stark, culturally atrophied life of the isolated farm and small towns." [25]

The interplay of giant power and regional planning constituted the central theme of a 1926 report of the New York State Commission of Housing and Regional Planning. Prepared by Henry Wright, it began with a familiar denunciation of the metropolitan culture which had drained the countryside of its population and vitality and contributed to a cycle of rising urban land values, intensive land utilization, and spiraling "overheads." Turning to the historical evolution of metropolitanism, Wright described the period prior to 1840 as one of eotechnic balance and diffusion, typified by "small, self-sufficing communities scattered throughout the State—each raising its own food and manufacturing the greater part of its own necessities." [26] Over the next four decades —"Epoch One"—two opposing tendencies proceeded simultaneously: a continued movement to the soil and an increasing amount of manufacturing centralized in the valley L which formed the backbone of the state. A critical event occurred in the decade 1870–80, when steam assumed the ascendancy over water power. This accelerated the tendency toward industrial concentration, for factories had to be built near the canals and railroads which carried their fuel. The widening of markets resulting from improved machinery and mass production hastened concentration in localities which claimed superior transportation facilities.

"Epoch Two," the decades following 1880, "witnessed a complete breakdown of the independent economic units that composed the State. The city became the dominant organism, supplemented by the specialized farm." [27] Local industry declined and total farm acreage decreased between 1880 and 1920. Factory plants increased in size and located primarily in the Mohawk-Hudson (L valley) system. Any hopes for a reversal of this centralization imposed by the railroad and steam engine lay in long-distance electric transmission and motor transportation. These could reshape the entire life of the State, assuming they were deliberately used to enhance the attractiveness of farm and town life, decentralize factory production, and distribute the advantages of the metropolis more equitably among the community units comprising the regional city.

Two years previous to Wright's report, MacKaye had urged a giant power policy designed to nurture an environment superior to the metropolitan—a regional reconstruction which would produce communities combining the virtues of the old colonial type and modern commercial type—and two years after Wright's report he presented in his *New Exploration* a philosophical, semi-mystical summation of regionalism. [28] By the "new exploration" MacKaye referred to the challenge posed by the "wilderness of civilization" in contrast to the "wilderness of nature" which had taxed the ingenuity of our ancestors. In the old exploration the key figures had been the explorer and scientist; those of the new exploration were the economist and engineer—co-workers in the "giant task of straightening out the tangle of civilization." The chief goal of regional engineering in the new exploration would be "control and guidance of industrial migration" in order to achieve an efficient balance of "resources, commodities, and environment."

Regional engineering succeeded or failed to the degree that it encouraged the growth of the "indigenous" environment at the expense of the metropolitan. The threefold indigenous or "elemental" environment consisted of the primeval, rural, and urban. MacKaye described the primeval as the "environment of life's sources," the rural as the environment of agriculture, self-sufficiency, and primary group association, and the urban as the environment of manufacturing, trade, specialization, and group organization. He saw no conflict between the rural and "real" urban, which was merely the village "grown up." Although the urban environment was too large for universal primary group association, it was small enough to constitute a true community in which the specialized interests and groups retained a "vital common interest in the common will."

The menace lay not in the urban environment, but in the metropolitan environment which had submerged and replaced the former by a "standardized massing of humanity void of social structure, unbound by geographic confines, and uninspired by any common interest. Intimate self-government is

being ironed out by generalized overhead administration. Mechanical standardization replaces human integration." Describing the metropolitan environment as an intruder, MacKaye proposed to
substitute the regional city: a grouping of villages
and cities, linked by giant power and motor trans-
port, and providing all the advantages of the
indigenous environment. Dissipating the "congealed
massing" of metropolitanism and unifying "work
and art and recreation and living," the regional city
offered opportunities for the fundamental relationships upon which the fullness and significance of
life depended: the primeval contact of man and
nature, the rural village's "generalized contact of
man and man," and the "specialized contact of
man and man" typical of the urban community.[29]

Chapter 7

BACK IN 1920 Frederick Ackerman had observed acidly that the American people's leading planning principle was, " 'I want what I want when I want it.' "[1] Controlled, cellular regional reconstruction, undermining the entire land, taxation, and investment structure of the urban metropolis and demanding an extraordinary level of social cooperation, discipline, and long-range planning, had little appeal or precedent in the United States. It would be a mistake to confuse the regionalism of the RPAA —more a philosophy of life than a detailed blueprint—with the regional planning which actually emerged in the 1920's. These differed in origin and objective. From the point of view of the RPAA, the regional planning of the 1920's represented "inorganic" city planning writ large. In sharp contrast to Wright's report on New York State, the regional planning of the 1920's confined itself largely to metropolitan areas or counties. The most influential regional planning scheme of the decade—the Russell Sage Regional Plan of New York and Its Environs

—evoked only the sharpest criticism from the RPAA.

The development of regional planning in the 1920's was closely associated with Thomas Adams, a Scottish architect and town planner who worked with Ebenezer Howard in advancing the Garden City movement in England. Serving as manager of Letchworth for several years, as town planning adviser to the Local Government Board of England between 1909–1914, and in a similar capacity for the Canadian government between 1914 and 1921, he reached the conclusion at an early date that the region constituted the basic planning unit. The logical order of progression, he insisted, was the regional survey followed by the regional plan and, last, the city plan. Municipal boundaries, Adams argued, represented administrative conveniences which possessed no functional significance in relation to the actual problems which planners confronted: industrial location, housing, transportation, power, water, waste disposal, park systems and other land uses. "The need for the control of land, the linking up of the urban centre with the agricultural district, the control of natural resources, the prevention of speculation, a wider outlook on the social aspects of city planning, the need for a scientific basis for surveys and plans," Adams explained, "all mean that more emphasis must be given to regional planning and development. . . ." [2]

The trustees of the Russell Sage Foundation selected Adams to head their Regional Plan, a project launched in 1921 which illustrated in particularly dramatic fashion the dissimilarity between the regionalism of the RPAA and the regional planning of the 1920's. It would be useful, however, to examine the general character and development of regional planning in the period before turning to the Russell Sage venture.

In the 1920's the automobile, as much as any other influence, awakened planners and others to the fact that city and surrounding country had been welded into a single functional unit. Facilitating movement in and out of the city, the auto provided a new mobility which created regional highway problems having little relation to political boundaries.[3] Yet the automobile represented in acute form only one of a series of problems which came to be recognized as regional in scope. Even before 1900 the expansion in the size and population of cities forced them to look beyond their political boundaries in order to cope with such challenges as water supply, waste disposal, and acquisition of open space for parks and recreation. One of the earliest regional responses occurred in Boston, where the establishment of specialized metropolitan commissions foreshadowed the authorities and districts of a later date. A Metropolitan Sewerage Commission was established in 1889, followed by a Metropolitan Water Board and a Metropolitan Park Commission in the 1890's. The Sewerage and Water agencies combined in 1901, and in 1919 all three were consolidated to form a Metropolitan District Commission. By the early 1920's, the specialized commission had become a common administrative form dealing with problems which vitally affected the city but which could not be controlled autonomously. These commissions flourished particularly in the New York metropolitan area, where they included a Metropolitan Sewerage Commission, a Passaic Valley Sewer Commission, an Essex, Union and Hudson County Park Commission, a Bronx Rivers Parkways Commission, a Palisades Interstate Park Commission, a New York Port Authority, and New York and New Jersey Bridge and Tunnel Commission.

The specialized nature of these commissions and their unsuitability for coping with most phases of regional land use led in the 1920's to a parallel development of public regional planning agencies. Although limited in power and scope, their mere existence confirmed the RPAA's contention that regional planning had become a functional necessity. Among the official regional planning commissions established were those in Los Angeles County, California (1923), Allegheny County, Pennsylvania (1923), Milwaukee County, Wisconsin (1924), Lucas County, Ohio (1924), Onondaga County, New York (1927), Glynn County, Georgia (1928), and Hamilton County, Ohio (1929). The Niagara Frontier Planning Board in New York (1925) and the Maryland-National Capital Park and Planning Commission (1927) spanned more than one county. A few additional public regional planning agencies appeared in the 1920's, but were limited to the protection of scenic beauty like the Santa Barbara County (California) Planning Commission, or never functioned like the Albany Capital District Planning Commission, or were adjuncts to municipal planning commissions and restricted largely to highway affairs.[4]

The public and private regional planning agencies of the 1920's (confined mostly to counties and metropolitan areas) often emphasized the need for comprehensive plans covering all phases of regional land-use. In practice, particularly in the case of public agencies, the planning did not extend much beyond roads, parks, and utilities. The work of the public agencies was frequently useful and constructive, but remote from housing or community planning. In Los Angeles, for example, a Regional Planning Conference preceding appointment of the official commission in 1923 excluded housing entirely from its calculations.[5] The Milwaukee County Regional Planning Department, created through the initiative of the County Park Commission, was established as a branch of the highway commissioner's office. Parks, highway platting, and zoning consumed much of its time. The Department was responsible for the enactment of a county zoning ordinance in 1927, one of the first in the country. It specifically disavowed that inclusion of an agricultural district under the ordinance implied a permanent greenbelt which precluded other uses in the future.[6]

The vigorous efforts of the Milwaukee County Regional Planning Department to develop a county park and parkway system suggest that along with the automobile a major stimulus to regional planning in the 1920's came from the long tradition of landscape architecture and municipal park planning. Referring to a tendency toward "extension and decentralization" exhibited by Milwaukee and most other American cities, the Department insisted

that "it is only a matter of reasonable foresight that
provision be made now for recreational areas thru-
out the county, since such areas can only be provided adequately and economically before the people
arrive in great numbers." It viewed the "naturalistic
park" as a "modern invention" which derived from
the work of Olmsted and Vaux at Central and
Prospect Parks, and the parks and parkways of
Boston designed by Olmsted and Charles Eliot.
Pointing to these and the parks of Minneapolis and
Kansas City as models for the integrated system it
proposed, the Department devoted considerable attention to surveys, plans, and construction of a
county park system.[7]

Along with the development of a "major thorough-
fare plan," the National Capital Park and Planning
Commission of Washington, D. C., included parks
and parkways among its highest priorities. It
adopted the McMillan Plan of 1901 as the basis of
a proposed park system and in 1930 succeeded in
acquiring a $23,000,000 appropriation for regional
park development. The Washington Commission
displayed an interest in social problems unusual for
the official regional planning agencies of the 1920's.
Influenced by the Chicago practice of grouping
various facilities—school, library, assembly hall—
around a park or playground area, it recommended
the establishment of ten or twenty such neighborhood centers in the District of Columbia.[8]

Following its establishment in 1927, the Maryland-National Capital Park and Planning Commission worked closely with the Washington Commission on matters of regional zoning and parks. The

Maryland organization, along with the Niagara
Frontier Planning Board, represented one of the few
instances of regional planning which transcended
county boundaries. Stein's Commission of Housing
and Regional Planning midwived the Niagara
Frontier. At a statewide conference on regional
planning in the spring of 1924, sponsored by the
Commission and addressed by Stein, a State Federa-
tion of Planning Boards was established. In the fall
of the same year, Governor Smith convened a meeting of municipal and county officials from Erie and
Niagara Counties to consider proposals for regional
planning in the area. Held at Tonawanda under the
auspices of the Commission, the conference established a Committee on Permanent Organization
which recommended the formation of a Niagara
Frontier Planning Association composed of officials
and private citizens. Encouraged by this support,
the Commission introduced into the legislature a
measure authorizing the creation of a Niagara
Frontier Planning Board and launched a campaign
to stimulate regional organization in the Albany
district.[9]

Established in 1925, the Niagara Frontier Planning Board consisted of the mayors of the six cities
and members of the boards of supervisors of Erie
and Niagara Counties. Possessing only advisory
powers, the Board included among its objectives the
improvement of land and water transportation in
the region, the development of a park and playground system, encouragement of local planning
and zoning, and efficient sanitary engineering aimed
at prevention of pollution and improved sewerage

disposal facilities. These were all commendable objectives, but quite different from the systematic regional reconstruction envisioned by the RPAA. Like that of its counterparts in the 1920's, the approach of the Niagara Frontier Planning Board represented magnified city planning. It responded, for example, to the problems created by the increase of auto and truck traffic by calling for the same program of road widening, new road construction, and "their better articulation" favored by municipal engineers and planners.[10]

Throughout the period under discussion it was not the RPAA, but rather Thomas Adams and the Russell Sage project which exerted the greater practical influence on regional planning development. Even before his association with the Russell Sage Foundation, Adams was described as a pioneer who had done more than any other person to popularize regional planning—the cooperation of communities "in the solution of their joint engineering and utility problems."[11] He was always respected by the members of the RPAA for his contributions to regional planning in Canada and his early connections with Letchworth, Howard, and the Garden City movement in England.[12] MacKaye had been impressed by Adams' Canadian work for city, town, and agricultural community, particularly his plans for township layout in which roads radiated from a community center and which provided for segregation of forest land and division of agricultural land into "farm allotments of efficient areas for family use."[13] Yet it was the RPAA alone which dissented from the chorus of acclaim which greeted the monumental product of

ten years' labor—the Regional Plan of New York
and Its Environs (RPNY).

Charles D. Norton, a banker associated with
Frederic A. Delano in the development of Burnham's
famous Chicago Plan, was the individual most
responsible for acquiring Russell Sage support for
the RPNY. Norton, who had served as chairman of
an Advisory Committee on the City Plan in New
York, had long wished to see Chicago's example
emulated in the eastern metropolis. The Advisory
Committee, appointed by George McAneny, president of the Board of Aldermen and a leading propo-
nent of planning and zoning in New York, had
proved to be a frustrating beginning. Norton's committee was supposed to advise a Committee on the
City Plan organized by McAneny in 1914 and con-
sisting of the five borough presidents. The City Plan
Committee never really functioned and in 1916 was
abolished by Mayor Hylan along with the Advisory
Committee.

Norton's first overtures to the Russell Sage Foundation were unsuccessful. Taking advantage of a
request by Robert W. de Forest that he study Foundation affairs and recommend new projects, Norton
prepared a memorandum in the winter of 1919
which urged sponsorship of a "plan bold enough to
visualize the commercial, the industrial, the social
and the artistic values and possibilities of our glori-
ous harbor and all of its broad and varied environs. . . ." [14] The idea at first seemed too costly to
execute and Norton was unable to persuade de
Forest and Alfred T. White, both trustees of the
Foundation, and John Glenn, its secretary, to trans-

late their early discussions into action. Persisting in his efforts, Norton finally converted White to his position. In the winter of 1920, White arranged a luncheon attended by de Forest, Glenn, Norton, and Nelson P. Lewis, Chief Engineer of the Board of Estimate and a prominent leader in the early city planning movement. This time de Forest agreed to a preliminary survey by Lewis beginning in the spring of 1921 and to official presentation of the proposal to the trustees. In February of 1921, the trustees authorized appointment of a committee and an initial expenditure of $25,000. The RPNY was officially launched in the spring of 1922, and the next year Adams was appointed general director of plans and survey.[15]

The RPNY ultimately cost over one million dollars. Its eight survey volumes, containing a wealth of data, represented the most comprehensive analysis ever undertaken for a metropolitan region. They covered 1) Major Economic Factors in Metropolitan Growth and Arrangement; 2) Population, Land Values and Government; 3) Highway Traffic; 4) Transit and Transportation; 5) Public Recreation; 6) Buildings: Their Uses and the Spaces about Them; 7) Neighborhood and Community Planning; 8) Physical Conditions and Public Services. *The Graphic Regional Plan: Atlas and Description* was published in 1929, and the summary volume by Adams, *The Building of the City,* appeared in 1931. The RPNY constituted a landmark in planning history for the collaboration in a single project of planners, architects, engineers, lawyers, economists, social workers, and other specialists. The Plan they devised, moreover, was significant for its practical influence. It was eminently successful, if measured by the number of proposals subsequently adopted by local government agencies. The Russell Sage Plan, finally, greatly stimulated the growth of both local and county planning organization in the Metropolitan Region. Particularly important in this respect was the Regional Plan Association, Inc., established in 1929 and still active.[16] These achievements, however, did not soften criticism of the Plan by members of the RPAA.

It is unnecessary to discuss here the statistical findings of the RPNY or its many specific proposals relating to trunk line railroads, suburban rapid transit, waterways and harbor improvement, parkways and boulevards, industrial, commercial, and park development, airports, and civic centers. It was not so much the statistical data or the specific projects which distressed the RPAA as the assumptions about the scope and purpose of regional planning which guided Adams and his collaborators in their preparation of the RPNY. The Plan seems to occupy a midway position between the throughgoing regionalism of the RPAA and the parks and roadways emphasis of the official regional planning agencies of the period. Its endorsement of the Neighborhood Unit idea of Clarence Perry, its effort to win support for a 60–40 ratio of open space to land coverage through zoning and street and park allocation, and its proposals for dispersion of industry and population to suburbs, sub-centers, and satellite cities all represented attempts to improve the quality of residential environments in the metropolitan area. Yet the RPAA, particularly Mumford, regarded it as contradictory, confused, and, ultimately, self-defeating.

Determined to produce a plan which would be adopted by local authorities, Adams deliberately stressed the need for moderation and practicality. "To assume that an existing city could be re-created or a new city built in some perfect form or logical geometric pattern," Adams asserted, "is to acknowledge ignorance of the rudiments of city growth in any condition of society that has ever existed." [17] He proposed neither a radical reorganization of the region, nor a complacent acceptance of existing density levels, subdivision practices, and zoning regulations. Adams insured that the unifying feature of the entire Plan would be a "diffused recentralization," meaning a balanced regional "distribution of land uses in relation to transportation, industry and residence," combined with a "well balanced distribution of bulks of building in relation to open areas." [18] Diffused recentralization broke down specifically into 1) industrial recentralization designed to lower density in existing congested centers and to create new centers; 2) residential diffusion resulting in the creation of compact residential neighborhoods throughout the region integrated with the industrial areas; and 3) a "sub-centralization" of business coordinated with industrial and residential development. The specific proposals of the Plan were devised with these ends in view.

Adams and his staff planned for an anticipated increase of population in the region from 10 million to 21 million by 1965. This estimate, based upon "careful study of past growth and existing trends," [19] brought into sharp focus the conflict between the RPAA and the Adams group. Because the latter limited their scope to a forty-mile radius of Manhattan and took for granted a tremendous increase of population in the metropolitan area, the RPAA felt that the group had failed to distinguish between a true plan and a spurious plan based upon projections of existing population trends and institutional arrangements. [20] The contrast, in the eyes of the RPAA, lay between Wright's slim 1926 report on a regional plan for New York State and the multi-volume projections of the RPNY. Admitting that the Russell Sage project resulted in a number of useful practical suggestions, Mumford nonetheless maintains that the "sort of outline for a larger order of planning, which went into the State Report of 1926, was the necessary complement to planning on a purely metropolitan scale, with all the limitations of local governments, and with all the incentives to maintain old levels of congestion." Mumford saw the entire RPNY as a failure in imagination, and as the expected product of a "very orthodox and conservative group, whose task was essentially to do the best possible with the existing political and economic forces and to suggest improvements and coordinations that would be immediately practicable." [21]

Mumford expressed his views in a scathing criticism published in the *New Republic* in 1932. Describing the area within a forty-mile radius of Manhattan encompassed by the Plan as a "purely arbitrary concept, based upon future possibilities of transportation and past facts of city growth," Mumford complained that "to assume that growth within an arbitrary metropolitan area will continue automatically in the future, under the same conditions that prevailed in the past, is to beg the whole question. . . ." [22] Despite the appearance of electric power, the automobile and the telephone, and new methods of corporate organization, he continued, the Plan lacked the awareness of alternatives to metropolitan centralization which appeared in Wright's report. Mumford raised the possibility that "effective planning" was impossible within the context of existing financial institutions, but he considered this to be no excuse for "evading the problem itself or for hiding the essential facts with illusory hopes and false promises." [23]

Getting down to particulars, Mumford objected to a wide range of proposals and omissions. He emphasized, for example, the Plan's failure to consider the forces influencing the balance of city and farm population, and the relationship between metropolitan growth and finance. Mumford complained also that the Plan might profitably have examined the relative efficiency of commercial row types as opposed to existing skyscraper construction. Adams' repeatedly expressed preference for a regional recentralization based upon lower population densities did not satisfy Mumford, who interpreted the Plan's proposals for Brooklyn's Columbia Heights, the upper East Side water front, the Manhattan civic center, and the entire lower Manhattan area as an attempt to maintain a high level of land and tax values based upon congestion. On the central issue of housing and residential environment,

Mumford commended the Neighborhood Unit idea of Clarence Perry, but added that the Plan failed to consider the means to implement it. Instead of depending upon "fitful and unreliable" limited-dividend companies, Mumford urged a unified approach to neighborhood-building, involving municipal land purchase to supply tracts, co-ordinated building, street and park development, and establishment of an administrative authority to carry out the projects.

Mumford maintained, as a general proposition, that all the highway and rapid-transit schemes outlined in the Plan comprised an alternative to, rather than a means toward, community-building. His own prescriptions for reconstruction of the New York region included dispersal of business from Manhattan, government sponsorship and financing of new cities outside the region toward which industry would be directed, and the reconstruction of slums and blighted areas combined with "intensive internal colonization" of population while it continued to increase within the metropolitan area.

The regionalism of Mumford and the metropolitan planning of Adams were virtually irreconcilable. In a reply to Mumford's criticisms, Adams defended the Plan's moderate progressivism as the only possible approach to the complexities of planning in a democratic society. As far as the distinction between a plan and a projection was concerned, Adams contended that the planner could not simply consider the way he wished a city to evolve, but had to "give consideration to the way it is evolving." Labelling Mumford as an "esthete-sociologist" who had not confronted the realities of democratic planning,

Adams insisted he preferred the evils which accompanied freedom to a "perfect physical order achieved at the price of freedom." He denied, in addition, that the Plan would fail to reduce congestion and pointed to its many proposals for low-density development in the environs.[24]

Conclusion

Mumford saw in the RPNY a grabbag of proposals, some desirable for purposes of immediate application, but when taken together nowhere approximating the systematic regional community-building which he envisioned. Although he has modified details, Mumford has consistently upheld the principles underlying the community-planning conception in the 1920's: "I would hold, even now, that the current methods of city growth, by treating each of its functions as independent, and so territorially at liberty to be set down anywhere, is a formula for urban disintegration, whether practiced on a small scale or a large one; by the same token, when urban growth is in order, it must proceed by packets or 'quanta' (neighborhoods, boroughs, cities) in which all of the necessary elements of urban life are present, not just those which are profitable or politically expedient." As to form and structure, Mumford adds, "there is plenty of room for differences over the nature of these quanta units—as to their area, population, density, their social and economic variety; and at no point did the RPAA ever have a rigid definition, except as a preliminary to action. Our very conception of regionalism was based on the recognition of variety and multiplicity. . . ." [25]

Like Thomas Adams, contemporary planners tend to accept metropolitan centralization and existing socio-economic institutions as realities which cannot be ignored or dismissed. This is not merely a defensive posture, but reflects a positive acceptance of metropolitanism as a worldwide phenomenon providing benefits otherwise unobtainable, at least in the same degree, for the great majority of people. Thus in outlining the objectives of metropolitan form, Kevin Lynch emphasizes above all those of variety and range of choice (goods, services, facilities) and a high potential for "personal interaction." Supplementary objectives include minimum initial and operating costs, comfort (with regard to climate, noise, indoor and outdoor space), provision for change and adjustment, and "imageable" structure. Lynch contends that neither a radical diffusion of population (dispersed sheet) nor a low-density bunching (galaxy of settlements) can satisfy most of these criteria: "A radical, consistent dispersion of the metropolis appears to restrict choice, impair spontaneous interaction, entail high cost, and inhibit a vivid metropolitan image. A galaxy of small communities promises better, but would still be substandard as regards choice, interaction, and cost, besides being harder to realize." [26]

Actually, none of the criteria outlined by Lynch in his excellent summary of the goals of metropolitan form conflict with those of the regional city conceived in the 1920's. In considerable measure, however, members of the RPAA rested their case on the concept of optimum urban size, contending that beyond a certain point the metropolis could no longer satisfy these criteria or at least achieve a satisfactory equilibrium. Defenders of metropolitanism maintain that the concept of optimum urban size is an act of faith rather than a demonstrated truth. A recent discussion of this complex issue by a sociologist yields only the most tentative conclusions. According to Otis Duncan, the "optimum size of cities is quite different from the standpoint of certain criteria from what it is on the basis of others. It is found that even an apparently unitary criterion— e.g., health—may give conflicting indications of the optimum. There is no immediately obvious way in which these various optima may be objectively equilibrated, compromised, weighted, or balanced to yield an unequivocal figure for *the* optimum population for a city." [27] On the basis of the available evidence, however, Duncan does not find that the small- or medium-sized city fares badly with regard to convenience and expenditure in transportation, health, public safety, municipal efficiency, education, communication facilities, public recreation, retail variety, civic association, and marriage and fertility rates. On the other hand, it would seem that some positive correlation prevails between the size of a city and cultural innovation and diffusion.

It should be clearly understood, whatever the vagaries of the issue, that the RPAA never maintained that any single optimum size could or should prevail. Members of the RPAA always viewed size in functional terms; it was not expressible as a unitary ideal or equilibrium, but as a relationship between population groupings and community objectives. The RPAA did not deny that cities of limitless size were technologically feasible or that, as matters stood, the metropolis did not offer advantages unobtainable elsewhere. Indeed, their complaint was that the centralization of so many intellectual, social, cultural, and commercial advantages in the metropolis served, in the end, to restrict choice and variety—probably the most important of all the criteria postulated both by defenders of metropolitanism and the RPAA. The paradox lay in the fact that in taking for granted the inevitability and desirability of metropolitan growth, planners and others involved in the decision-making process devoted inordinate attention and resources to the physical needs of the metropolis, whatever the consequences for the regional hinterland. The result of this narrowing in the range of vision, successful as it may have been in keeping the metropolis in operation, was a failure in nurturing alternative community-types, thus limiting the boundaries of genuine choice and diversity in life-styles for the majority of people. In the regional city to which the RPAA aspired there was room not only for the large city but for the widest range of community-types offering the widest choice of life-styles and the least desecration to the countryside.

The posing of this alternative to metropolitan centralization, combined with innovations in site-planning and housing finance, represent the outstanding contributions of the RPAA. It was unique in its broad view of urban form and environment as a product of residential planning adapted to the social needs of a modern urban population, of financial mechanisms able to compensate for the structural inadequacies of building and lending agencies, and of a regional planning directed to the nurture of a multiplicity of community types.

The RPAA's career as an organized group ended around 1933, although individual members have remained active to the present. Mumford attributes the demise to a combination of circumstances, including a lack of influence over President Roosevelt, a scattering of homes and jobs, the transfer of his own and Wright's attention to the Housing Study Guild, which they had established in 1933 in conjunction with Albert Mayer, and, most important, the inability of the New York inner circle to get members in other cities to foster sub-groups. In 1948 an attempt was made to revive the RPAA through formation of a Regional Development Council, resulting in a few years of discussion but little more.[28]

Mumford doubts that the loose, informal character of the RPAA affected either its influence or durability for the worst. Its influence, he suggests, "cannot be measured in any quantitative scale," while in its anti-formalism the RPAA "counteracted the over-attachment to mere organization and established the at least equal value of 'gemeinschaft.'" As far as attracting younger men to the group and stimulating sub-groups outside of New York City were concerned, Mumford doubts that a "full time secretary and a large mailing list would have helped, or would have furthered our program measurably." [29] Yet *gemeinschaft* has its limitations in an organized world of competing power structures, particularly in the crucial transition from ideas to the realm of politics and administration, and for all it contributed to the vitality of the RPAA, it was undoubtedly at least partially responsible for its short life, and may have restricted its long-term influence. It was precisely when the RPAA functioned as an organized group, however informal, and acted through other organized groups—the Committee on Community Planning of the American Institute of Architects, the New York State Commission of Housing and Regional Planning, the City Housing Corporation—that unusually rapid progress was made in closing the gap between community planning as a cause or ideal and community planning as an administered function of society.

Notes

1. "Report of Homestead Commission," *Massachusetts House Documents,* No. 198, 1910, 1.
2. *Ibid.,* 5–7; Freeman M. Saltus, "Minority Report," *Massachusetts House Documents,* No. 258, 1910, 2; *Massachusetts House Documents,* No. 1687, Mar. 17, 1910, May 13, 1910, 1.
3. Augustus L. Thorndike took the place of Arthur B. Chapin in 1913. Added to the Commission in the same year were Cornelius A. Parker, a Boston lawyer, and Arthur C. Comey, a Cambridge landscape architect. Only three further changes occurred in the personnel of the Commission. Professor George Chandler Whipple of Harvard superseded Clement F. Coogan, George A. Bacon replaced Charles F. Gettemy, and Walter L. McMenimen substituted for Sterling when he left for war duty in Washington in 1918.
4. "Homesteads for Workingmen," Massachusetts Bureau of Statistics, *Labor Bulletin No. 88,* Jan. 1912, 7.
5. "Report of the Homestead Commission," *Massachusetts House Documents,* No. 2000, Jan. 1913, 37, 42.
6. "First Annual Report of the Homestead Commission," *Public Document No. 103,* 1913, 16. The Commission was also responsible for the establishment of a Conference of Massachusetts Planning Boards. Among the publications it issued to encourage planning were Home-

stead Commission, "Information and Suggestions for City and Town Planning Boards," *Bulletin No. 2,* Nov., 1914; and Arthur C. Comey, "A Schedule of Civic Surveys," *Bulletin No. 5,* May, 1916.

7. "Third Annual Report of the Homestead Commission," *Public Document No. 103,* 1915, 7.

8. "First Annual Report," 49, 48, 75.

9. Warren D. Foster, "The Massachusetts Homestead Commission," National Conference of Charities and Correction, *Proceedings,* 1912, 422.

10. "Third Annual Report," 42.

11. Homestead Commission, "Teaching Agriculture to Families as a Relief for Unemployment and Congestion of Population," *Bulletin No. 3,* Jan. 1915, 4; "Third Annual Report," 9, 73.

12. "Homesteads for Workingmen," 23.

13. The Commission's findings on foreign aid-to-housing appear in "Homesteads for Workingmen" and "First Annual Report." The data on Australia and New Zealand is drawn from these sources. For additional information on foreign aid-to-housing see Edith Elmer Wood, *The Housing of the Unskilled Wage Earner: America's Next Problem* (New York, 1919), and U. S. Department of Labor, Bureau of Labor Statistics, "Government Aid to Home Owning and Housing of Working People in Foreign Countries," *Bulletin No. 158,* 1915.

14. "Third Annual Report," 1915, 72.

15. Homestead Commission, "The Lowell Homestead Project: Description, Explanation and List of Questions," *Bulletin No. 7,* rev., Dec. 1917, 5.

Chapter Two

1. The federal war housing experiment is discussed in Roy Lubove, "Homes and 'A Few Well Placed Fruit Trees': An Object Lesson in Federal Housing," *Social Research,* XXVII (Winter 1960), 469–86.

2. Statistical data is drawn from: Office of the Administrator, National Housing Agency, "Housing After World War I: Will History Repeat Itself?" *National*

Housing Bulletin No. 4 (Washington, D. C., Oct. 1945). Useful also on post-World War I housing costs is National Industrial Conference Board, "The Building Situation," *Special Report No. 29, July 1924.*

3. John Irwin Bright, "The Building Industry in the United States," *Journal of the American Institute of Architects,"* VIII (Aug. 1920), 308; Commission of Immigration and Housing of California, *Seventh Annual Report,* Jan. 1921, 20; Ritchie Lawrie, Jr., "Approaching the Housing Problem with a State-wide Program," *The Housing Problem* (papers presented at the state conference of the Massachusetts Chamber of Commerce, Boston, Feb. 18, 1920), 5; "Report of the Housing Committee of the New York State Association of Architects," *Journal of the American Institute of Architects,* VIII (Dec. 1920), 431; City and Suburban Homes Company, *Twenty-Third Annual Report of the President,* May 1919, 6, 7. The postwar housing shortage and its implications are considered also in: "The Need for New Houses," *Independent,* XCIX (Sept. 20, 1919), 390–92; W. H. Ham, "Lessons for Housing Work in Bridgeport," National Housing Association, *Proceedings,* VIII (1920), 95; Lawson Purdy, "Exemption from Taxation and Other Subsidies," *ibid.,* 3–18; Alfred E. Smith, "A Housing Policy for New York," *Survey,* XLV (Oct. 2, 1920), 3–4; Arthur Gleason, "Houses: The Need," and "The Lack of Houses: Remedies," *Nation,* CX (Apr. 17, 1920, Apr. 24, 1920), 511–13, 546–49; Luther H. Gulick, "Attacking the Housing Problem," *Survey,* XLIII (Mar. 20, 1920), 76–65; R. P. Blake, "America's Housing Need and How to Meet It," *American City Magazine,* XXIII (July 1920), 26–30; Henry R. Brigham, "How to Meet the Housing Situation," *Atlantic Monthly,* CXXVII (Mar. 1921), 404–13; John Ihlder, "The Housing Situation," National Conference of Social Work, *Proceedings,* 1922, 278–81; Samuel Untermeyer, "Who Is Responsible for the Housing Shortage?" National Housing Association, *Proceedings,* IX (1923), 19–29.

4. Bleecker Marquette, "The Human Side of Housing: Are We Losing the Battle for Better Homes?" National Conference of Social Work, *Proceedings,* 1923, 344.
5. Philadelphia Housing Association, *Housing in Philadelphia,* 1921, 3, 17, 27, 35.
6. Milwaukee Housing Commission, *Report,* Nov. 30, 1918, 3, 5.
7. "State Housing," *Housing Betterment,* VIII (Sept. 1919), 83; "Municipal Housing Declared Unconstitutional," and "Urges Municipal Housing for Boston," *ibid.* (Dec. 1919), 38–39, 43; "Municipal Housing for Patterson," *ibid.,* IX (Feb. 1920), 46–47; Daniel J. Cosgro, "City of Cohoes to Build Houses for Sale to Its Citizens," *American City Magazine,* XXXI (Sept. 1924), 201. On Louisiana see Edith Elmer Wood, *Recent Trends in American Housing* (New York, 1931), 239–40 (hereafter cited as Wood, *Recent Trends*), and *Monthly Labor Review,* XV (Aug. 1922), 161.
8. State of California, *Report of the Commission on Land Colonization and Rural Credits* (Sacramento, 1916), 5.
9. S. James Herman, "Homes for Veterans," *Survey,* LXII (July 15, 1929), 453. The Durham and Delhi Settlements are discussed in Wood, *Recent Trends,* 246–50, and an account of Durham appears in Benton MacKaye, *Employment and Natural Resources: Possibilities of making new opportunities for employment through the settlement and development of agricultural and forest lands and other resources* (Washington, D. C., 1919), 109–12.
10. John Taylor Boyd, Jr., "Recent Developments in Housing Finance," *Architectural Record,* XLVIII (Nov. 1920), 427.
11. Edith Elmer Wood, "Using Postal Savings Funds," National Housing Association, *Proceedings,* IX (1923) 125, 126.
12. Edith Elmer Wood, "How to Get Better Houses," *Journal of Home Economics,* XIX (Feb. 1924), 67.
13. On the Borland-Pomerene Bill see, Wood, *The Housing of the Unskilled Wage Earner,* 227–28.

Chapter Three

1. "Report of the Committee on Community Planning," *Proceedings of Fifty-eighth Annual Convention of the American Institute of Architects*, 1925, 114.
2. Lewis Mumford, "Attacking the Housing Problem on Three Fronts," *Nation* CIX (Sept. 6, 1919), 333.
3. Letters from Lewis Mumford to author, Aug. 14, 1961, and Feb. 7, 1962.
4. The biographical data on Mr. Stein is drawn from an Interview, Mar. 3, 1962, a typed Vita given to the author, and a Letter, June 26, 1962.
5. Interview with Clarence S. Stein, Mar. 3, 1962.
6. Letter from Lewis Mumford to author, Feb. 7, 1962.
7. "Housing Conditions," *Report of the Housing Committee of the Reconstruction Commission of the State of New York*, Mar. 26, 1920 (Albany, 1920), 4.
8. *Ibid.*, 6–7, 9, 12.
9. *Ibid.*, 45.
10. Federal, state and local efforts to control rents during World War I are discussed in Edward L. Schaub, "The Regulation of Rentals During the War Period," *Journal of Political Economy*, XXVIII (Jan. 1920), 1–36. Besides New York, such states as New Jersey, Colorado, Wisconsin, Massachusetts, Delaware, Maine, and Illinois attempted to control rentals in some way during the postwar housing crisis. See Marcus Whitman, "The Public Control of House Rents," *Journal of Land and Public Utility Economics*, I (July 1925), 343–61. Some measure of rent control lasted in New York State until 1929. The laws did not apply to new dwellings. A recent discussion of the tax exemption measure is contained in Committee on Tax Policies, Citizens' Housing and Planning Council of New York, *How Tax Exemption Broke the Building Deadlock in New York City* (May 1960).
11. *Report of the Commission of Housing and Regional Planning*, Dec. 22, 1923 (Albany, 1924), 34. Hereafter cited as *Report*, CHRP. . . .

12. State of New York, *Report of the State Board of Housing,* Mar. 9, 1927 (Albany, 1927), 48, 51.
13. *Ibid.,* 25.
14. Clarence S. Stein, "Housing New York's Two-Thirds," *Survey,* LI (Feb. 15, 1924), 510, and "A New Venture in Housing," *American City Magazine,* XXXII (Mar. 1925), 277–78; Lewis Mumford, "Houses—Sunnyside Up," *Nation,* CXX (Feb. 4, 1925), 115.
15. "Report of the Committee on Community Planning," *Proceedings of the Fifty-sixth Annual Convention of the American Institute of Architects,* 1923, 106.
16. John Irwin Bright of Philadelphia preceded Stein as chairman of the Committee, which was formed in 1919. At the time it issued its first report under Stein's leadership in 1922, it consisted of Bright, Frederick L. Ackerman, Edward H. Bennett, Frederick Bigger, Charles H. Cheney, M. H. Goldstein, Carl F. Gould, Thomas G. Holyoke, H. Olin Jones, Henry F. Withey, and Henry Wright. Among its members later in the decade were William T. Johnson, Rudolph Weaver, E. B. Gilchrist, and F. R. Walker.
17. Letter from Clarence S. Stein to author, Apr. 19, 1961.
18. Letter from Lewis Mumford to author, Feb. 7, 1962.
19. *Ibid;* Letter from Lewis Mumford to author, Feb. 12, 1962.
20. Interview with Clarence S. Stein, Mar. 3, 1962.
21. Letter from Lewis Mumford to author, Feb. 12, 1962.
22. Clarence Perry, a staff member of the Russell Sage Foundation and formulator of the Neighborhood Unit principle of urban design, exerted a particularly direct influence upon the RPAA. Letter from Lewis Mumford to author, Oct. 12, 1962. On Perry see Roy Lubove, "New Cities for Old: The Urban Reconstruction Program of the 1930's," *The Social Studies,* LIII (Nov. 1962), 203–13.
23. Letter from Lewis Mumford to author, Mar. 12, 1962.
24. Letter from Lewis Mumford to author, Sept. 22, 1962; Interview with Clarence S. Stein, Nov. 12, 1962.
25. Letter from Lewis Mumford to author, Oct. 12, 1962.

26. Interview with Clarence S. Stein, Mar. 3, 1962.
27. *Ibid.*
28. Letter from Lewis Mumford to author, Oct. 12, 1962.
29. Frederick L. Ackerman, "Where Goes the City Planning Movement? V. Drifting," *Journal of the American Institute of Architects,* VIII (Oct. 1920), 353.
30. Letter from Lewis Mumford to author, Sept. 18, 1962.
31. Letter from Lewis Mumford to author, Mar. 7, 1962. The 1925 report was in two parts, Part I being a repetition of the 1924 report of the Committee on Community Planning.
32. "Report of the Committee on Community Planning," *Proceedings of the Fifty-eighth Annual Convention of the American Institute of Architects,* 1925, 114, 115.
33. *Ibid.,* 115–16, 118.
34. *Ibid.,* 122.
35. *Ibid.,* 113, 121.

Chapter Four

1. Interview with Clarence S. Stein, Mar. 3, 1962.
2. Raymond Unwin, *Nothing Gained by Overcrowding,* 3rd ed. (Garden Cities and Town Planning Association, 1918). Unwin later applied a similar analysis to vertical overcrowding in "Higher Building in Relation to Town Planning," *Journal of the Royal Institute of British Architects,* XXXI, 3rd ser. (Jan. 12, 1924), 125–40.
3. Raymond Unwin, *Town Planning in Practice: An Introduction to the Art of Designing Cities and Suburbs* (London, 1920 [1st ed. 1909]), 164.
4. John Taylor Boyd, Jr., "Garden Apartments in Cities," *Architectural Record,* XLVIII (Aug. 1920), 124–28, 131–34.
5. Important precedents for Thomas's work can be traced to the 1890's. Even then, New York architects like Ernest Flagg and I. N. Phelps Stokes were emphasizing the economic, design, and site-planning superiority of large building groups and subdivisions in contrast to the 25 x 100 commercial lot.

6. State of New York, *Final Report of the Joint Legislative Committee on Housing* (Albany, 1923), 16. The Joint Legislative Committee was responsible for a 1922 measure authorizing insurance companies to invest a sum not exceeding 10 per cent of their total assets in housing operations.

7. The Bayonne work is described in Andrew J. Thomas, *Industrial Housing* (Bayonne, N. J.: Bayonne Housing Corporation, 1925), and John Taylor Boyd, Jr., "A Step Towards Slum Clearance: The Garden Tenement of the Empire Mortgage Company on the East Side of New York," *Architectural Record,* LVII (Mar., 1925), 208–11, which also deals with the Avenue A project. The Bayonne, Avenue A, and Thomas Garden Apartments are discussed in Victor H. Lawn, "House, for the Goose, House for the Gander," *Survey,* LVII (Dec. 15, 1926), 371–73, 412. On model tenements and garden apartments in the 1920's, see also Wood, *Recent Trends,* 209–14, 221–28.

8. Andrew J. Thomas, "Is It Advisable to Remodel Slum Tenements?," *Architectural Record,* XLVIII (Nov. 1920), 417–24; Frederick L. Ackerman, "Climbing the Greased Pole," *Journal of the American Institute of Architects,* IX (Nov. 1921), 361; Interview with Clarence S. Stein, Mar. 3, 1962.

9. Letter from Lewis Mumford to author, Feb. 7, 1962.

10. Interview with Clarence S. Stein, Mar. 3, 1962. Like Stein, Bing belonged to the Ethical Culture Society. Dissatisfied with commercial success alone, he had been anxious for some time to "do something useful." Interview with Charles S. Ascher, May 14, 1963.

11. Alexander M. Bing, Henry Wright, Clarence S. Stein, "Preliminary Study of a Proposed Garden Community in the New York City Region," unpublished MS (1923) in the possession of Mr. Stein, 25, 26.

12. *Ibid.,* 26.

13. *Ibid.,* 34. They pointed, however, to what they considered serious limitations in the war housing: the tendency to

choose locations to serve war ends rather than broad housing purposes, the pressures of speed in influencing planning and execution, the limited innovations in site-planning and subdivision with an eye to future sale of the developments in small units.

14. Bing, Wright and Stein, "Study of a Proposed Garden Community," 12.
15. Letter from Lewis Mumford to author, Feb. 7, 1962.
16. Letter from Lewis Mumford to author, Feb. 12, 1962. Bing was somewhat surprised that Sunnyside needed extensive publicity and promotion—he had assumed that its virtues were self-evident. Interview with Charles S. Ascher, May 14, 1963.
17. Clarence S. Stein, *Toward New Towns for America* (New York, 1957), 44, 47–48.
18. The Radburn differentiated street system, however, was not directly influenced or inspired by Central Park, although Stein lived across the street from it. Interview with Clarence S. Stein, Mar. 3, 1962.
19. Collaborating at Radburn with Stein and Wright were Frederick L. Ackerman, James Renwick Thomson, and Andrew J. Thomas. Ralph Eberlin was the site engineer.
20. Interview with Clarence S. Stein, Mar. 3, 1962.
21. Benton MacKaye, "The Townless Highway," *New Republic,* LXII (Mar. 12, 1930), 93–95.
22. "Report of the Secretary and Treasurer of the Regional Planning Association, on Activities of the Association Since the Meeting June 17, 1926," RPAA, Minutes, Apr. 13, 1927, 2. A copy of the RPAA Minutes are in the possession of Clarence S. Stein.
23. "Summary of Discussions of Problems Connected with a Garden City, at a Series of Conferences of the Regional Planning Association of America at the Hudson Guild Farm," RPAA, Minutes, Oct. 8 and 9, 1927. In relation to community organization, the new contract and lease system devised ultimately by Charles S. Ascher and Louis Brownlow and the origins of the "Radburn

Association" are discussed in Charles S. Ascher, "The Extra-Municipal Administration of Radburn," *National Municipal Review,* XVIII (July 1929), 442–46.

Chapter Five

1. At Sunnyside the City Housing Corporation had benefited from the "unearned increment" on the extra land it had purchased surrounding the development. The same tactic failed at Radburn because of the depression and resulting deflation of land values. Interview with Charles S. Ascher, May 14, 1963.
2. A brief description of housing trusts appears in Wood, *The Housing of the Unskilled Wage Earner,* 92–93. On the Charlesbank Homes see Frank Chouteau Brown, "The Low-Rental Apartment—An Economic Fallacy," *Architectural Record,* LVI (July 1924), 69.
3. Abraham Goldfeld, *The Diary of a Housing Manager* (Chicago: National Association of Housing Officials, 1938).
4. U. S. Department of Labor, Bureau of Labor Statistics, "Cooperative Movement in the United States in 1925 (Other than Agricultural)," *Bulletin No. 437,* Miscellaneous Series (Washington D. C., Mar. 1927), 90, 91.
5. Lemuel Shattuck, *Report of the Sanitary Commission of Massachusetts, 1850* (Cambridge, Mass., 1948), 208.
6. Telephone conversation with Clarence S. Stein, Feb. 21, 1962.
7. Letters from Lewis Mumford to author, Apr. 2, 1961, Aug. 14, 1961.
8. Clarence S. Stein, "The New York Puzzle," *Journal of the American Institute of Architects,* XII (Feb. 1924), 84.
9. Interview with Clarence S. Stein, Mar. 3, 1962.
10. Clarence S. Stein, "Amsterdam—Old and New," *Journal of the American Institute of Architects,* X (Oct. 1922), 327, 320.
11. *Report, CHRP,* Dec. 22, 1923 (Albany, 1924), 35; *Ibid.,* Mar. 6, 1925 (Albany, 1925), 29, 21. Along with

Stein, the Commission consisted of Sullivan W. Jones,
state architect; Arthur W. Brandt, commissioner of
highways; James A. Hamilton, industrial commissioner;
Oliver Cabana, Jr.; Mrs. Sara Conboy; Peter D. Kier-
nan; and Chauncy J. Hamlin. Its staff, directed by
George Gove, included A. F. Hinrichs and F. O. Billings.
Gove later served as secretary of the New York State
Board of Housing.

12. *Report, CHRP,* Feb. 22, 1926 (Albany, 1926), 37.
13. Letter from Lewis Mumford to author, Feb. 12, 1962.
14. *Report, CHRP.,* Feb. 22, 1926 (Albany, 1926), 48.
15. *Ibid.,* 49.
16. Governor Smith had transmitted two special messages to
the legislature in support of the Commission's plan.
Democrats prepared bills incorporating a State Housing
Bank, but the Republican alternate bill omitting the Bank
was ultimately successful. See "Subsidized Housing for
New York," *Housing Betterment,* XV (June 1926), 73–
93.
17. Louis H. Pink, who succeeded Darwin R. James as chairman of the State Housing Board, maintained later that
useful as the New York Law was in demonstrating
what could be achieved with government aid, the restrictions imposed on the private developer and the limited
inducements of tax exemption offered little prospect for
slum clearance and building on a large scale. Louis H.
Pink, Reminiscences, Columbia University Oral History Project, 36, 37.
18. A recent study points out that "despite the large expansion of Federal aids in the last twenty-five years
and despite the continued extension and improvement
of the terms on which homes are made available with
Federal credit aid, it is apparently true that the private
housebuilding industry serves only a fraction of the
American public." Martin Meyerson, Barbara Terrett,
William C. Wheaton, *Housing, People and Cities* (New
York, 1962), 254.
19. The Board consisted of Darwin R. James, chairman,
Oliver Cabana, Jr., John Halkett, Louis H. Pink, Aaron

Rabinowitz, and Sullivan W. Jones. Its secretary was George Gove.

20. *Preliminary Report of the State Board of Housing,* Dec. 15, 1926 (Albany, 1926), 16.

21. The projects are described in the State Board of Housing reports beginning in 1928. See also, Wood, *Recent Trends,* 264–71. In addition, two commercial firms, attracted by the benefits of the State Housing Law in a period of depression, sponsored three projects.

22. *Report of the State Board of Housing* (Albany, 1930), 13.

23. Meyerson, Terrett, Wheaton, *Housing, People and Cities,* 136, 264, 340.

24. *Report of the State Board of Housing,* Mar. 6, 1929 (Albany, 1929), 25, 26. A. E. Kazan, president of the Amalgamated Credit Union and Amalgamated Housing Corporation, was the outstanding leader in the development of its housing work.

25. Benton MacKaye, *The New Exploration: A Philosophy of Regional Planning* (New York, 1928), 68.

Chapter Six

1. Letter from Lewis Mumford to author, Apr. 2, 1961.

2. Hedwig Hintze, "Regionalism," *Encyclopedia of the Social Sciences,* XIII (1934), 208–18; Lewis Mumford, *Technics and Civilization* (New York, 1934), 291–92; Carlton J. H. Hayes, *France: A Nation of Patriots* (New York, 1930), 292–317.

3. Patrick Geddes, *Cities in Evolution: An Introduction to the Town Planning Movement and to the Study of Civics* (London, 1915), 74.

4. *Ibid.,* 143, 198.

5. *Ibid.,* 211.

6. By way of qualification, Mumford contends that Geddes never regarded the analogy as literal. Letter from Lewis Mumford to author, Sept. 10, 1962.

7. Lewis Mumford, "The Fate of Garden Cities," *Journal of the American Institute of Architects,* XV (Feb. 1927), 37, 38.

8. Lewis Mumford, "Regionalism and Irregionalism," *Sociological Review*, XIX (Oct. 1927), 277–88; "The Theory and Practice of Regionalism," *ibid.*, XX (Jan. 1928, Apr. 1928), 18–33, 131–41.

9. MacKaye's personal background and experiences are discussed in Lewis Mumford's introduction in Benton MacKaye, *The New Exploration: A Philosophy of Regional Planning* (Urbana, Illinois, 1962).

10. George Perkins Marsh, *The Earth as Modified by Human Action*, rev. ed. (New York, 1885), 33, 47–48.

11. Nathaniel S. Shaler, *Man and the Earth* (New York, 1905), 2, 8.

12. MacKaye, *Employment and Natural Resources*, 18.

13. Benton MacKaye, "An Appalachian Trail: A Project in Regional Planning," *Journal of the American Institute of Architects*, IX (Oct. 1921), 329.

14. "Report of the Committee on Community Planning," *Proceedings of the Fifty-fifth Annual Convention of the American Institute of Architects*, 1922, 102; *Ibid., Proceedings of Fifty-sixth Annual Convention*, 1923, 106.

15. Letter from Lewis Mumford to author, Feb. 7, 1962; RPAA, Minutes, June 12, 1923.

16. "Report of the Secretary and Treasurer of the Regional Planning Association, on Activities of the Association Since the Meeting June 17, 1926," RPAA, Minutes, Apr. 13, 1927.

17. Letter from Lewis Mumford to author, Sept. 18, 1962.

18. Lewis Mumford, "The Regional Community," 129, and Clarence S. Stein, "Dinosaur Cities," 138, *Survey*, LIV (May 1, 1925).

19. Stuart Chase, "Coals to Newcastle," 146, and Lewis Mumford, "Regions—To Live In," 152, *ibid.;* Lewis Mumford, "Architecture and Broad Planning. II. Realities vs. Dreams," *Journal of the American Institute of Architects*, XIII (June 1925), 199. Besides the articles cited, the Regional Plan Number of the *Survey* included: "The Fourth Migration," by Mumford; "Our Stake in Congestion," by Frederick L. Ackerman; "The

New Exploration: Charting the Industrial Wilderness," by Benton MacKaye; "Seeing a State Whole," by Alfred E. Smith; "Giant Power—Region-Builder," by Robert W. Bruère; "The Road to Good Houses," by Henry Wright; "Garden Cities: What They Are and How They Work," by C. B. Purdom; "Can We Have Garden Cities in America?" by Alexander M. Bing; and "Two-Generation Communities," by Joseph K. Hart.

20. Lewis Mumford, "The Intolerable City: Must It Keep on Growing?" *Harper's Magazine,* CLII (Feb. 1926), 288.

21. Giant Power Survey Board, *Report to the General Assembly of the Commonwealth of Pennsylvania* (Harrisburg, Pa., Feb. 1925), 26, 27, 17–18; Philip P. Wells, "Our Federal Power Policy," *Survey,* LI (Mar. 1, 1924), 570. In the mid-1920's, the most intensive electric power development existed on the West coast, where a high-tension, long-distance transmission system stretched 1,200 miles from California to Oregon.

22. "Message of Transmittal," Giant Power Survey Board, *Report,* xi, xii. Like Pinchot, Governor Smith of New York favored a giant power policy under public ownership or tight control. Alfred E. Smith, "The Stake of the Public," *Survey,* LI (Mar. 1, 1924), 574–76.

23. Sir Adam Beck, "Ontario's Experience," *ibid.,* 585–90, 650–51. The Hydro-Electric Power Commission of Ontario, formed in 1906, represented a partnership of municipalities with each community contributing in proportion to services.

24. Robert W. Bruère, "Pandora's Box," *ibid.,* 647. Mumford was another who cited Ontario as a model for socially-oriented giant power: a balanced day-night load transmitted through the same main, requiring a "community devoted to both domesticity and industry" in contrast to the city-suburban disjunction. "The Intolerable City," 290.

25. Robert W. Bruère, "Giant Power: Region-Builder," *Survey,* LIV (May 1, 1925), 161–88.

26. *Report, CHRP,* May 7, 1926 (Albany, 1926), 17.
27. *Ibid.,* 35.
28. In 1924, MacKaye had urged a giant power policy aimed at creating an "efficient environment" characterized by self-comprehensibility, use of modern industrial technics, population of "democratic proportions," compactness as opposed to isolation and congestion, access to attractive environs, modern sanitation, and unity. The "old colonial type," MacKaye claimed, lacked only modern sanitation and technology, the modern commercial type lacked all but these. "Appalachian Power, Servant or Master?" *Survey* LI (Mar. 1, 1924), 618.
29. MacKaye, *New Exploration* (1928), 68.

Chapter Seven

1. Frederick L. Ackerman, "Where Goes the City Planning Movement? IV. The Confusion of View-Points," *Journal of the American Institute of Architects,* VIII (Aug. 1920), 286.
2. Thomas Adams, "City Planning and City Building," *Journal of the American Institute of Architects,* IX (June, 1921), 197, and Adams, "Regional and Town Planning," National Conference on City Planning, *Proceedings,* 1919, 77, 87, 88.
3. Sidney D. Waldon, "Superhighways and Regional Planning," National Conference on City Planning, *Planning Problems of Town, City, and Region,* 1927, 152; Howard Strong, "Regional Planning and Its Relation to the Traffic Problem," American Academy of Political and Social Science, *Annals,* CXXXIII (Sept. 1927), 215.
4. Theodora Kimball Hubbard and Henry Vincent Hubbard, *Our Cities To-Day and To-Morrow: A Survey of Planning and Zoning Progress in the United States* (Cambridge, Mass., 1929) depicts briefly regional planning development to that date in Chap. IV, 46–64. See also Harlean James, "The Cost of Regional Planning," *Journal of Land and Public Utility Economics,"* V (Aug. 1929), 303–10; George B. Ford, "Regional and

Metropolitan Planning: Principles, Methods, Co-operation," National Conference on City Planning, *Proceedings,* 1923, 1–32.

5. *Conclusions of the Regional Planning Conference of Los Angeles County, California at Glendale* (Sept. 16, 1922). The work of the Los Angeles County Regional Planning Commission is discussed in Hugh R. Pomeroy, "Regional Planning in Practice," National Conference on City Planning, *Proceedings,* 1924, 111–28, and Pomeroy, "Two Years of Regional Planning in Los Angeles County," *City Planning,* I (Apr. 1925), 47–49.

6. Milwaukee County Park Commission and Milwaukee County Regional Planning Department, *Annual Report,* 1927, 35.

7. Milwaukee County Regional Planning Department, *Annual Report,* 1924, 15, 20. The Department, if not concerned with garden cities, was conscious of the need for relating its highway and park work to improved subdivision and site-planning. It recommended the J. C. Nichols development in Kansas City, Shaker Heights in Cleveland, and, especially, Radburn, as models. *Biennial Report,* 1929 and 1930, 45, 46.

8. National Capital Park and Planning Commission, *Annual Report for the Fiscal Year Ended June 30, 1927,* 9, 10, 11; *Ibid., Annual Report for the Fiscal Year Ended June 30, 1929,* 12, 23. One contribution of the Commission to the improvement of housing conditions was the employment of John Ihlder to study and report on the chronic problem of Washington's alley slums. See *Annual Report for the Fiscal Year Ended June 30, 1930,* 26 ff.

9. *Report, CHRP,* Mar. 6, 1925 (Albany, 1925), 64–67. The Commission was responsible for a New York State law of 1925 authorizing the creation of advisory regional planning boards. The Niagara Frontier, however, was established by authority of a special statute.

10. Niagara Frontier Planning Board, *Second Annual Report,* 1926, 12. On the Niagara Frontier and for a more general analysis of the administrative basis of regional

planning see Howard E. Long, "The Planning Organization of the Niagara Frontier Region," National Conference on City Planning, *Planning Problems of Town,
City, and Region,* 1927, 141–49.

11. Morris Knowles, "Engineering Problems of Regional
Planning," National Conference on City Planning,
Proceedings, 1919, 115, 116.

12. Letter from Lewis Mumford to author, Feb. 12, 1962.

13. MacKaye, *Employment and Natural Resources,* 20, 116.

14. Committee on the Regional Plan of New York and Its
Environs, *The Plan of New York, With References to the
Chicago Plan* (Letter from Charles D. Norton to
Frederic A. Delano) (New York, 1923), n.p.

15. The original Committee on the Regional Plan included
Charles D. Norton, chairman, Robert W. de Forest,
Frederic A. Delano, John M. Glenn, Dwight W. Mor-
row, and Frank L. Polk. Frederick P. Keppel served as
secretary, and Flavel Shurtleff as assistant secretary.
Delano succeeded Norton upon his death in 1923.

16. On progress in implementing the RPNY, see Staff of the
Regional Plan Association, Inc., *From Plan to Reality*
(New York, 1933).

17. Thomas Adams (assisted by Harold M. Lewis and
Lawrence M. Orton), *The Building of the City,* Regional Plan (New York, 1931), II, 105.

18. *Ibid.,* 138. Also, Thomas Adams, "The Goals and Snags
in Regional Planning," National Conference on City
Planning, *Planning Problems of Town, City and Region,*
1929, 39.

19. Staff of the Regional Plan, *The Graphic Regional Plan:
Atlas and Description,* Regional Plan (New York,
1929), I, 312.

20. Letter from Lewis Mumford to author, Feb. 12, 1962;
Interview with Clarence S. Stein, Mar. 3, 1962.

21. Letter from Lewis Mumford to author, Mar. 12, 1962.
If the plan was practical and conservative, however, it
was not entirely because of the sponsorship. Adams, its
"heart and center" was himself determined to produce
an action-oriented plan (unlike, presumably, Henry

Wright's alluring but ineffectual proposals for regional reconstruction in New York State). Interview with Lawrence M. Orton, May 17, 1963.

22. Lewis Mumford, "The Plan of New York, I," *New Republic,* LXXI (June 15, 1932), 123.

23. *Ibid.,* 124.

24. Thomas Adams, "In Defense of the Regional Plan," *New Republic,* LXXI (July 6, 1932), 208, 209.

25. Letter from Lewis Mumford to author, Sept. 10, 1962.

26. Kevin Lynch, "The Pattern of the Metropolis," *Daedalus: Journal of the American Academy of Arts and Sciences,* XC (Winter 1961), 95.

27. Otis D. Duncan, "Optimum Size of Cities," in Paul K. Hatt and Albert J. Reiss, Jr., eds., *Cities and Society: The Revised Reader in Urban Sociology,* 2nd ed. (Glencoe, Illinois, 1957), 772.

28. Letters from Lewis Mumford to author, Apr. 6, 1961, Mar. 12, 1962.

29. Letter from Lewis Mumford to author, Mar. 12, 1962.

Index

19/10?